W9-BWU-240

Photo: Jean Bockelman

 *LATINOAMERICANA EDITORES*

COLECCIÓN: PALABRAS AL VIENTO

Sponsored by the School of Liberal Arts and Sciences of
Western Oregon State College.

ISBN 0-9640795-1-8

Printed in the United States of America

Eduardo González Viaña

Frontier
Woman

La mujer de la frontera

**LATINOAMERICANA
EDITORES**

COLECCIÓN: PALABRAS AL VIENTO

Un asombroso narrador

*La magia de E. González Viaña no viene volando, sino
paso a paso a través de la frontera que no se acaba nunca y
del sueño que se la traga.
Pocos viajeros han pasado por la tierra en que caminan los
personajes
de este asombroso narrador.
Rulfo fue uno.
Fantasía de dioses, brujos, fantasmas y nahuales que
vencen a la Migra en los pasos de la tierra de nadie.
La eternidad alumbra en la palabra de una anciana que no
permite la muerte de su hijo e imparte instrucciones a los
caminantes sin fronteras.
Pequeño gran milagro es "La mujer de la frontera."*

**Fernando Alegría
Stanford University**

Foreword

At Western Oregon State College, during the spring of 1994, I asked my Latin American Culture students to complete a community service task as part of their requirements for the class. The task consisted of helping "Hispanic" families from the Willamette Valley, in Oregon, as tutors in many areas that ranged from literacy and the learning of basic English to the study of driving regulations, the history of America, the manner in which to appear before the judicial system, and other necessary skills for their survival and integration into mainstream the U.S.

It may seem strange, but, before this experience, most of my students confessed that never in their lives had they spoken a word to a native Spanish speaker. Something similar occurred with the people we helped. Most of them are seasonal workers from Mexico or Central America whose economic resources are limited. Also, they generally live in the same urban sector, shop in the same stores, and receive services in Spanish. As a result of all this, their contact with English speakers is limited and at times stamped with reciprocal distrust.

But of course, this distance is not only present in the two linguistic communities mentioned above. For an observer, it's amazing, and almost unbelievable, to discover that in the United States, in the same space and time, so

many different ethnic groups can coexist without ever even acknowledging each other completely. I can say this, because through my simple interviews, I have noticed something that any poll at a larger scale could prove: that even the perceived physical characteristics between one group and another are not exact, but, rather generally, a stereotype. To talk about a "Hispanic" race is a good example of this.

For all these reasons, it could be gathered that the first encounter between students and immigrants would be somewhat timid, but it was not so. After an initial and mutual icebreaker, all estrangement was left behind, and one as well as the other began communicating as if they had always been together. After the second week of work, my most optimistic predictions were surpassed. I will now tell you how and why. During the month prior to the course, after some door to door work, I had selected twenty-five families that would be visited two hours a week by twenty-five students.

Twenty-five is not a magic number, it is the maximum number for classes at WOSC. Rather than this limit, I had thirty-five enrollees. On their behalf, the "Hispanic" families invited two or three other families to these reunions. At the end, there were a few hundred people involved in the project, and they would somehow find in a small living area, or poor but generous dining room, space that they would convert into their classroom.

And my students did not back down: two hours a week was their obligation, but most preferred to do three. For most of them, the established friendly bond increased greatly the number of visits, and the motives were as varied as a birthday, a wedding, a juvenile party, and even an

exchange of invitations to their respective churches amongst people that practiced different religions. Maybe they discovered that, they really were not that different, or that God usually sits in the same chair next to them.

Let us rid ourselves of this prolog quickly. We have repeated the feat during the winter of '94 and the current spring of '95. The result my student's effort can be told better than I can. It will be told every day by many people who can now read road signs and can now write love letters.

At my request, my students have written papers that summarize their experience, some of which I have published here. On my behalf and thanks to the support from Dr. John P. Minahan, Dean of Liberal Arts and Sciences, and from Dr. Richard S. Meyers, former Western President, I continued with the project and wrote a monograph about the Hispanic population of the Willamette Valley.

Nonetheless, at editing time, I told myself that for now I would save that paper, and bring to light some testimonies from my students. Instead of the monographic text, I publish a story that I have recently written in Oregon, "Frontier Woman", whose main character, Doña Asunción, can tell many things about the human family, not only about those of Hispanic ancestry.

As in all tales, half of the story was told to me and the other half I dreamt. Maybe that is how it happened, or maybe it was the other way. The third half only God knows.

Eduardo González Viaña

Resurrection Sunday, Easter, 1995
Corvallis, Oregon

Acknowledgments

*F*rom shore to shore and from soul to soul, my students are building a bridge. Thanks to them and thanks to Dr. John Minahan, Dean of Liberal Arts and Sciences of Western, who has strongly supported this multicultural task.

The translation of La Mujer de la Frontera has been done by a group of enthusiastic students: Melody Richardson, Martín Martínez, and Betsy Simpkins who were led by Lisa George. My friends Brenda Mc Cullough of Oregon State University, Pat Oliver and the fiction writer Mark Fettke reviewed the translation.

The students Richard Vallejos and Silvia Gomez typed the testimonies and finally Sue Payton took care of the edition.

Cristina and Antonio Cornejo-Polar, my publishers, cannot deny some responsibility.

Thanks to Mercedes, my mother. She knows why.

Contents

I have set before you life and death,
blessing and cursing:
therefore choose life...

Deuteronomy 30:19

La mujer de la frontera
Frontier Woman

Caminan y caminan desde anoche, pero todavía no han llegado a la cumbre. Caminando en la forma que caminan, podrían ser alcanzados por un rayo y seguir caminando sin saberlo. Todos los que partieron con ellos se encuentran ya al otro lado desde hace varias horas, pero el hombre y la mujer avanzan con mucha dificultad, y a veces se quedan inmovilizados en la arena sin poder dar un paso más cuando ya está a punto de amanecer sobre la frontera sur de los Estados Unidos.

-Ya no doy más- dice él.

-Anda, ya estamos a punto de llegar. Ya falta poco.

-Es que no puedo sacar la pierna de aquí. Esto parece arena movediza.

-Tú sabes que solamente es un cerrito. El último cerrito de México. ¿Te acuerdas de anoche? La primera en pasarlo fue una señora embarazada. Después ha pasado todo el mundo. Incluso, muchos niños. ¿Te acuerdas? ¿Te acuerdas de cuando partimos?... Anda, no es hora de echarse para atrás. Me dijiste que te ibas a portar bien

- Pero usted sabe que yo no puedo, que ya no doy más.

Frontier Woman
La mujer de la frontera

They have been walking and walking since last night, but still haven't reached the summit. Walking the way they are and because they are in a hurry, they could be hit by lightning and they would keep on walking without noticing. All those who left with them have already been on the other side for hours, but the man and the woman advance with much difficulty, and sometimes they remain immobilized in the sand, not able to take even one more step as the sun is just about to rise on the southern border of the United States.

"I can't go on any longer," he says.

"Come on, we're almost there. It's not much further."

"It's that I can't take my leg out from here. This seems like quick sand."

"You know it's only a little hill. The last little hill of Mexico. Do you remember last night? The first one to pass was a pregnant woman. Since then, the whole world has passed. Including many children. Do you remember? Do you remember when we left? Come on, this is not the time to turn back. You told me you were going to behave."

-Descansa un ratito, y después seguimos la marcha.

-Es que no puedo sacar la pierna del hoyo donde la he metido. Este cerro me está devorando.

-Deja que yo te voy a jalar, y cuando ya estés afuera, te echarás sobre mi manta, y dormirás un rato hasta que tomes fuerzas...

Arriba se borran lentamente los luceros, y entra una luna amarilla que se va como si se fuera para siempre, y por fin, cuando el sol comienza a volar sobre la última montaña de México, su luz descubre a esta pareja sobre la cumbre. Ahora ya es posible distinguir que la mujer, una anciana enjuta pero enérgica, quizás cercana a los ochenta años, tiene de un brazo al hombre, aparentemente enfermo, y lo lleva arrastrando hacia el otro lado de la colina, por el costado donde se encuentran los Estados Unidos de América.

-Vas a ver que cuando lleguemos allá, te vas a sentir bien. Y te vas a curar de todos tus males. Vas a ser otro.

El hombre parece animarse, y da algunos pasos más resueltos. Advierte que han pasado la cima, y ya se encuentran descendiendo el otro lado de la montaña de arena. Entonces salta y comienza a correr hacia allá abajo como si fuera un niño. Al choque del viento, está a punto de volar la venda blanca que le cubre la frente, pero el tipo se la asegura y continúa el feliz descenso. Un rato más tarde se detiene y bruscamente se queda inmovilizado como si estuviera viendo en el horizonte a un ángel con una trompeta. Cuando la dama llega hasta él y lo toma del brazo, sacude la cabeza con desaliento.

"But you know that I can't, I can't go on any longer."

"Rest a little while, and later we'll continue the walk."

"It's that I can't take my leg out of this hole. This mountain is devouring me."

"I'm going to pull you, and when you're out, you will fall onto my lap and sleep awhile until you gain some strength."

Half an hour later, when the sun begins to fly over the last mountain of Mexico, its light discovers the couple on the summit. Now it is possible to distinguish that the woman, old but energetic and slender, about eighty, has on her arm the man, who is apparently sick. She's pulling him towards the other side of the hill, to the side where they would find the United States of America.

"You'll see when we get there, you are going to feel fine. And you're going to be cured of all your ailments. You're going to be a new person."

The man seems inspired and takes a few more steps. He notices that they have passed the summit, and they are already descending the other side of the mountain of sand. He leaps and starts to run down there as if he were a child. At the crash of the wind, he is at the point of taking off the white bandage that covers his forehead, but instead he tightens it and continues the happy descent. A while later he stops abruptly and is immobilized as if he were seeing an angel with a trumpet on the horizon. When the woman reaches him, she takes him by the arm, but he shakes his head in dismay.

-Ya no me sostenga, mamá. Creo que ya no es necesario- dice mientras señala un punto en el horizonte. Allá abajo se divisa un grupo humano al que todavía no puede distinguir completamente, de modo que igual podrían ser los agentes norteamericanos o los "coyotes" a quienes pagaron para que los ayudaran a cruzar la frontera.

Manuel Doroteo Silveira Martínez, en Guatemala, acababa de cumplir cincuenta años cuando tuvo el primero de aquellos inaguantables dolores de cabeza. Le duró un día, pensó que se trataba de una "perseguidora" y se propuso no beber nunca más como lo había hecho el día de su cumpleaños. El segundo lo sorprendió en la oficina donde trabajaba como contador, y esa vez lo llevaron en una ambulancia al hospital. Pasada la emergencia, el médico que lo había atendido lo convenció de que debería quedarse en el hospital para que se le hiciera un chequeo completo.

Viudo y sin hijos, inmensamente solo en el universo, Doroteo tenía que avisar a su madre que iba a internarse en el hospital. En otra ocasión, habría evitado darle a conocer la mala nueva, pero esta vez era necesario decírselo porque de otra forma habría de notar su ausencia: solía visitarla cada tarde en el otro lado de la ciudad de Guatemala, donde vivía acompañando a una nieta casada, y por ello una repentina ausencia del hijo la habría aterrado.

Esa fue la razón por la cual doña Asunción Martínez de Silveira lo acompañó al hospital, conoció al médico, hizo amistad con aquél y con las enfermeras y supo lo que el paciente nunca llegaría a saber, a través de los sucesivos diagnósticos que el

"Don't hold me up anymore, Mother. I don't think it's necessary anymore- he says as he points to a spot on the horizon. There below one can see a group of people that still cannot be distinguished completely, so they could equally be the North American agents or the "coyotes", whom they paid to help them cross the border.

Manuel Doroteo Silveira Martínez had just turned fifty years old when he had the first of those unbearable headaches in Guatemala. It lasted a day, and after that he thought it had something to do with a hangover and that he would never drink like he had the day of his birthday. The second one surprised him in the office where he worked as an accountant, and this time they took him by ambulance to the hospital. The emergency passed, the doctor that had attended him convinced him that he should stay in the hospital for a complete physical.

Widowed and without children, immensely alone in the universe, Doroteo had to advise his mother that he was going to admit himself into the hospital. On another occasion he would have avoided worrying her, but this time it was necessary to tell her because she would notice his absence: he used to visit her every afternoon on the other side of the city of Guatemala, where she was living with her married granddaughter.

That was the reason that doña Asunción, the mother, knew, before he did, about the successive diagnoses the doctor had been disclosing to her. "A brain tumor... We don't know what kind of tumor... We could have to operate on him but we don't know what could happen". That was also the motive for her

médico le fue revelando: "Un tumor en el cerebro... No se sabe qué clase de tumor... Tendríamos que operarlo, pero no sabemos lo que pasaría." Y ése fue también el motivo por el que doña Asunción abandonó a la familia con la que vivía, y se fue a cuidar a su hijo.

-Pobre muchacho. No puedo dejarlo solo porque me necesita.- dijo, y a lo mejor agregó que ella no podía darse el lujo de continuar envejeciendo ahora, en aquellas circunstancias.

-Por favor, comprendan, voy a tener que dejarlos para cuidar a mi Doroteo.

Su nieta y el esposo de aquélla no querían dejarla partir, pero no pudieron impedirlo cuando la vieron salir dispuesta a luchar por la vida de su hijo, olvidada de la vejez, vestida toda de blanco, erguida y silenciosa como caminan las almas.

"Morirse y estar muriéndose no da lo mismo."- Doroteo no supo nunca quien había dicho eso porque la frase se le coló en el oído en los pasillos del hospital. Después, pensó que era una expresión carente de sentido. Al final, se dijo que en todo caso no le estaba dirigida porque él todavía no había pensado en que podía morir. En realidad, no podía enterarse de la verdadera naturaleza de su mal porque en América Latina no se suele comunicar ese tipo de diagnóstico a los pacientes terminales, sino a algún familiar autorizado. Alguna vez, alguien le informó que se trataba probablemente de un tumor benigno, pero más de eso no. Al cabo de dos años y luego de penosas radiaciones, el médico supo que ya no había nada qué hacer y que, probablemente, ya había pasado su turno.

to abandon the family she lived with and to go take care of her son.

"Poor boy. I can't leave him alone because he needs me," she declared and added that she couldn't allow herself the luxury of growing old if her son had such delicate health. So, overnight she stopped being an old woman and transformed herself into a nurse.

"Please, understand that I'm going to have to leave you, in order to take care of my Doroteo" she said to her granddaughter, who didn't want to let her leave, when she left home ready to fight for the life of her son.

In reality, Doroteo never was told the actual nature of his ailment. Doctors in Latin America usually don't communicate that to their terminal patients. One time he was told that it was probably a benign tumor, but nothing more. At the end of two years and after painful radiation treatments, his doctor knew that there was nothing he could do for him. Doroteo's time had probably come.

"Now you can leave the hospital. Outside you are going to feel better" the doctor told Doroteo. "Now you can do whatever you want with your life" he added, but he didn't let him know that he only had a few months left to live.

Doña Asunción heard him say it, but she didn't believe the doctor because night after night while she watched the Doroteo sleep, she read some popular magazines that talked about marvelous cures. Finally the "Readers Digest" and her own decision to believe in life convinced her that the only way to save her son was to take him to the United States.

-Ya puede irse del hospital. Allá afuera, se va a sentir mejor- le dijo a Doroteo. -Ahora puede usted hacer lo que quiera con su vida -añadió, pero no le hizo conocer que le quedaba poco tiempo.

A doña Asunción sí se lo dijo. "Le doy tres o cuatro semanas, y a lo mejor durante ese tiempo va a sentirse perfecto, como si estuviera sano, porque así es la enfermedad y así también es la muerte. A veces le da ánimos al enfermo para que se muera despacio, sin impaciencia de morir." Lo escuchó, pero no le creyó porque, noche tras noche, mientras cuidaba los sueños de Doroteo, se había dado tiempo para leer, en los pasillos del hospital, algunas revistas populares en las que se hablaba de curas prodigiosas. Al final, "Selecciones del Reader's Digest" y su propia decisión de creer en la vida la convencieron de que la única forma de salvar a su hijo era llevarlo a los Estados Unidos.

Cuando el paciente salió del hospital, brillaba en él ese aire saludable que suele dar la muerte a sus próximos huéspedes para que vivan felices el tiempo que les resta. La enfermedad parecía haberse ido, y sólo una completa calvicie, fruto de las radiaciones, podía delatar su estado, pero Doroteo se sentía animado y dispuesto a bromear.

-Realmente estoy guapo. Debe ser que me voy a morir- dijo en son de broma, aunque no le salió ese tono, sino uno como de miedo, y bruscamente supo que si no hacía algo iba a caer en cama otra vez. Pero no tuvo tiempo de deprimirse porque doña Asunción Martínez de Silveira ya tenía preparado el programa de todo lo que debían hacer a partir de ese momento para lograr la curación definitiva, y la receta era

When the patient left the hospital, in him shone the healthy air that Death usually gives to her next guests, so that they may live happily in the time they have left. The sickness seemed to have gone, and only complete baldness, a consequence of the radiation, could give away his condition.

"Actually, I'm attractive. It's probably that I'm going to die", he said jokingly, but suddenly he realized his tone was not humorous; but rather, it was fearful. He knew that if he didn't do something, he was going to end up in bed again.

But he didn't have time to get depressed because Mrs. Asunción Martinez Silveira already had prepared a plan for everything they should do from this moment on in order to achieve a definitive cure. And they didn't have a minute to lose. First of all, they would get the passports and go to the American Embassy to get visas.

Stubborn at first, but later obedient and finally sure, Doroteo followed his mother from one place to another and began to live his last days as if in all his life he had never possessed anything more than hope.

"But, shave son. You have to look real good so that the gringuitas will like you! You don't know how I would like a gringuita as a daughter-in-law!"

The Consulate said no. But mother and son wasted no time. It had taken them five hours to enter the diplomatic building, stand in lines and finally, after the interview, receive a negative answer. In only one hour, they had already bought two Mexican passports, and thanks to these papers, they were in Mexico City two weeks later. At the end of the third week, they were in Tijuana.

sencilla: viajarían a los Estados Unidos. Por lo tanto, no tenían un minuto que perder, y lo primero que iban a hacer era conseguir los pasaportes e ir a la embajada para conseguir la visa de ingreso.

Renuente al comienzo, pero obediente después, y por último seguro, Doroteo siguió de un lado a otro a su madre y comenzó a vivir los últimos días que le quedaban como si toda la vida no hubiera poseído otro bien que la esperanza.

-Pero aféitate, hijo. Tienes que ponerte buenmozo para que les gustes a las gringas. !No sabes cómo me gustaría tener una nuera güerita!

El Consulado dijo que no. Pero madre e hijo no perdieron el tiempo. Les había tomado cinco horas entrar al edificio diplomático, hacer algunas colas y, al fin, luego de la entrevista, recibir la negativa. Saliendo de allí, en solamente una hora, ya habían comprado dos falsos pasaportes mexicanos que les permitirían entrar sin problemas en ese país.

Dos semanas más tarde estaban en México DF, y al final de la tercera llegaban a Tijuana. Después de haber viajado cinco mil kilómetros en diferentes autobuses, ya se sabían de memoria el olor y el color de los caminos de México. En la frontera, contratar un "coyote" había sido una tarea sencilla, pero iniciar el tránsito no lo era. Todos los contrabandistas de gente ya estaban comprometidos con otros y les pedían esperar un mes, pero un mes era demasiado. Un mes equivale a un mes para una persona adulta y sana, no para una anciana ni para su hijo condenado a muerte. Pagaron más, pero al cabo de solamente dos semanas estaban atravesando la frontera por el lado que da a San Isidro. Y justamente allí estaban cuando Doroteo

At this moment, after traveling 5,000 kilometers in different buses, they knew by color, flavor and smell the maps of Mexico. Contracting a "coyote" was a simple task, but initiating the passage was not. All of the coyotes told them that they should wait a month because they were already committed to other groups of people. But one month was too much for them. One month equals one month for a sane, adult person, but not for an old lady and her dying son. They paid more, but at the end of just two weeks, they were crossing the border on the side that faces San Isidro. And that's right where they were when Doroteo managed to pass over the peak and see a group of strange people.

logró pasar de la cima y avistó un grupo de gente extraña.

Cuando Doroteo divisó al grupo humano en la playa, ya hacía largo rato que su madre los estaba viendo pero no le había dicho nada a fin de no preocuparlo. En vez de hacer eso, ella rezaba una oración al Espíritu Santo gracias a cuyo poder habían logrado llegar a la cima y avanzar hacia el otro lado del cerro. En ese momento, un hombre, de los que estaban abajo, comenzó a llamarlos agitando los brazos. Su voz todavía no llegaba hasta esa altura , pero sus movimientos enérgicos implicaban una orden de que se dieran prisa en bajar.

Madre e hijo se comenzaron a mirar entonces, el uno al otro, como lo habían hecho durante una época ya lejana, la infancia de Doroteo, en que las palabras quizás todavía no habían sido inventadas.

-Tiene usted razón, mamá. No tenemos de qué asustarnos. A ver si a lo mejor resultan ser las ánimas del Purgatorio que han venido a ayudarnos.

Durante el par de kilómetros que les faltaba para llegar hasta la gente, el enfermo caminó con agilidad como si nunca se hubiera sentido mal, e imaginó que los agentes federales eran comprensivos y amables, y los devolverían a Guatemala sin llamarles la atención. Por su parte, doña Asunción comenzó a pensar que el próximo intento para entrar en los Estados Unidos

When Doroteo could finally clearly make out the group of people on the beach, his mother had already been watching them a long time, but she had not said anything so as to not worry him. Instead of that, she continued praying to the Holy Spirit, thanks to whose power they had managed to arrive at the summit, from which they were now descending. At that moment, a man, one of those from below, began to call to them, waving his arms. His voice had still not reached them at their height on the hill, although his energetic movements implied an order that they hurry down.

Then the mother and the son began to look at each other as they had done during a time now distant- the infancy of Doroteo- in a time when words perhaps had not yet been invented.

"You're right, mother. We don't have to be scared. We'll see. The best thing would be that they turn out to be the souls in Purgatory who have come to help us."

During the final couple of kilometers that remained between them and the group of people, the sick man walked with agility as if he had never been sick. He imagined that the federal agents were going to be friendly and understanding by returning them to Guatemala without calling attention to them. Doña Asunción began to think that their next attempt to enter the United States was going to be simpler: they

sería más sencillo: tomarían un avión directo hacia Canadá, y de allí nomás se pasarían a Nueva York.

¿Cuánto costaría un pasaje, o más bien dos, desde Guatemala hasta Montreal? ¿Y desde allí, luego? ¿cómo serían los hoteles en la Tijuana del Canadá? ¿Y los cerros de esa frontera? ¿serían tan arenosos y desérticos como éste que acababan de pasar? ¿Sería fácil encontrar allí unos coyotes? ¿ y cuánto cobrarían esos caballeros? Calculó que en esos momentos les quedaban doscientos ochenticuatro dólares con cincuenta centavos y prefirió pensar en la moneda de su país, porque así resultaban con más dinero. Además, se dio cuenta que todavía no era necesario preocuparse por esas nimiedades. Venían huyendo de la muerte, y ya la habían dejado bien atrás.

Después de haberla visto con tanta frecuencia en sus vecindades, la muerte ya le resultaba bastante familiar. La anciana la había sorprendido conversando con algunos viejos conocidos suyos, la presentía volando por los dormitorios y las iglesias, la sabía gobernando con sabiduría su inmenso reino de sueños. Lo que no podía entender de ella era ese afán de querer llevarse al muchacho. La próxima vez, la encararía de mujer a mujer, pero no estaba muy segura de que aquéllo ocurriría muy pronto. "La pobre debe estar muy lejos: todavía debe andar preguntando por nosotros en Guatemala."

"Pero eso sí, si me encontrara con ella la atajaría para decirle: pongase usted en mi caso, señora, porque usted también debe tener hijos. Recuerde usted que son los hijos los que generalmente entierran a los padres, y no al revés. Así que no me ponga en el trajín de llevar al cementerio al único hijo

would take a plane directly to Canada, and from there they would go on to New York.

How much would one fare be, or rather two, from Guatemala to Montreal? And from there, later on? What would the hotels be like in the Tijuana of Canada? And the hills near that border? Would they be as sandy and barren as the ones they had just crossed over? Would it be easy to find some "coyotes" there who would guide them over the border? And how much would these men cost? She calculated then that two-hundred eighty-four dollars and fifty cents remained, though she preferred to think in the currency of her own country because that way they were rich. The mother realized that it was still not necessary to worry about these trivialities. They were fleeing from Death, and they had already left her well behind.

After having seen Death frequently, doña Asunción had already found her familiar enough. She had surprised Death conversing with some of her old acquaintances, and the old woman had imagined seeing Death flying through bedrooms and churches before, and she knew Death was, with wisdom, ruling over her great kingdom of dreams. What doña Asunción was not able to understand was Death's great desire to carry away her boy. The next time she would see Death, she would face her woman to woman, but she wasn't sure that this would happen very soon. "The poor thing must be very far away; she must still be inquiring about us in Guatemala."

She wasn't going to see her very soon, but if she saw her, she would stop her in order to tell her: "Put yourself in my shoes, Lady, because you must also

que tengo. Y, por otra parte, si quiere usted cambiar de difunto, hágalo. Lléveme a mí porque más bien va resultando que ya es mi turno, pero eso sí, déle un poco de tiempo al muchacho para que se reponga. Que si no el pobre no va a tener cuerpo para mi velorio."

Por supuesto que le diría eso, y seguro que la muerte le daría la razón, y acaso hasta enmendaría la equivocación que había estado a punto de cometer y le pediría mil disculpas y le echaría la culpa de sus errores a la naturaleza de su trabajo y a lo solita que andaba por esas inmensidades del cielo, pero doña Asunción tendría el tacto de evitarle tantas excusas y le cerraría la boca con algún comentario apropiado sobre lo bonitas que son, vestidas de negro, las mujeres pálidas de pelo largo.

Vencido y resignado, pero casi feliz, Doroteo seguía caminando hacia el grupo de extraños. Serena como un espíritu, su madre no terminaba de pensar en la muerte cuando advirtió que uno de los hombres, el que parecía ser el jefe, se adelantaba al resto y avanzaba hacia ellos. Ya estaba a unos cien metros de distancia y, a contraluz, no era posible vérsele el rostro, pero sí las huellas que sus pies iban dejando sobre la arena caliente. Entonces, la mujer advirtió que esas huellas avanzaban en dirección de Doroteo, y corrió a interponerse entre los dos hombres. Pero el gesto no fue necesario porque una voz amistosa comenzó a decir en cristiano:

-Ustedes son los de Guatemala, y los estamos esperando desde anoche. No, qué remolones habían resultado ser los de Guatemala... Y usted debe ser don Doroteo, pero se nota a la legua que le falta un

have children. Remember that the children are usually the ones who bury their parents, and not vice-verse. So therefore don't force me to transport the only son that I have to the cemetery. And, on the other hand, if you wish, we can make a deal for me to take his place. Take me instead of Doroteo, because it should be my turn . However, do give the boy a little time with me so that he might recover, because if you take me now, the poor boy isn't going to have the strength for my wake."

That's what she would say to her, and she was sure that Death would tell her that she was right. Perhaps she would correct the mistake that she had been at the point of committing, and she would apologize and lay the blame for her errors on her heavy work load and on the lonely one who traveled through the great vastness of the sky, but doña Asunción would have the tact to avoid Death's many excuses and would shut her mouth with some appropriate commentary, appealing to Death's vanity, about how pretty women dressed in black are, particularly pale women with long hair.

Conquered and resigned, but almost happy, Doroteo kept walking toward the group of strangers. Unruffled, his mother did not stop thinking about death even when she noticed that one of the men, the one who appeared to be the boss, was moving ahead of the others and advancing toward them. Now he was close to 100 meters away and, against the light, it was impossible to see his face, but, she could see the footprints that his feet were leaving in the hot sand. Then, the woman noticed that these footprints were advancing toward Doroteo, and she ran to put herself

tequila para ponerse en forma. Nosotros estamos aquí para llevarlos hasta la ciudad... ¿Cómo que no sabe quiénes somos?... Nosotros somos los coyotes del otro lado.

Lo dijo así, de costado, como si no dijera nada. Ya eran las seis de la mañana, y había tanta luz sobre la tierra que Doroteo y su madre conversaban mirando hacia el cielo, como cegados por la felicidad.

-¿Y nos puede decir, más o menos, como cuánto camino falta para llegar a los Estados Unidos?

-¿Cuánto camino? ¿Cómo que cuánto camino? Fíjese bien en la tierra, y aprenda a diferenciarla por el color porque no todas las tierras son iguales. Ustedes ya están caminando sobre tierra de los Estados Unidos.

Lo supo por boca del coyote, y allí nomás comenzó a mejorar Doroteo. Y también allí nomás se escuchó la pregunta de su madre:

-¿Y sabe usted, por si acaso, dónde vive el mejor doctor de los Estados Unidos?

Luisa Lane acababa de morir, y Clark Kent no sabía qué hacer, débil y casi humano, frente a la inflexibilidad del destino. En un cine de Los Angeles, al día siguiente de llegar, Doroteo y doña Asunción compartían el mismo silencio dolido con un

between the two men. But this gesture was not necessary because a friendly voice began to say in Spanish:

"You are the ones from Guatemala, and we've been waiting since last night. No, the slow ones from Guatemala have arrived. And you must be don Doroteo. Take note that only a little bit farther there's tequila to help put you back in shape. We are here to take you up to the city. We are the coyotes from the other side. "

He said it aside as if he hadn't said anything. It was already six in the morning, and there was so much light over the land that while Doroteo and his mother, looking toward the sky, were talking with the coyote, it was as if they were blinded by happiness.

"And can you tell us, more or less, how far it is to the United States?"

"How far? How far is it? Look well at the dirt, and learn to distinguish it by the color because not all land is equal. You already are walking on the land of the United States."

Once Doroteo found that out from the coyote, he began to get better right then and there. And there, he also heard his mother's question:

"And do you know, by chance, where the best doctor in the United States lives?"

corpulento acompañante, el coyote que los había guiado desde la frontera y que se había empeñado en ofrecerles albergue en su casa. Su nombre completo era Gabriel Angeles, pero sus amigos lo llamaban el Angel Gabriel.

-No, qué ocurrencia, guárdese el dinero- le había dicho a la anciana. -Ya otros pagarán, y, más bien, ustedes tienen que venir a quedarse en mi casa en Los Angeles porque de ninguna manera les voy a permitir que se vayan. Además, no sabe usted cuánto se parece a mi abuela que fue la que me crió y que debe estar ahora mismo revoloteando, con el mismo pelo blanco y las mismas manos largas de usted, allá arriba en el reino de los cielos.

El Angel Gabriel era soltero, pesaba unas doscientas cincuenta libras y había nacido en Guanajuato. Muy niño había perdido a sus padres en un accidente y, más tarde, a la muerte de su abuela, había partido hacia el norte para probar suerte: de eso hacía quince años y, ahora, de treinta, no se podía quejar porque hablaba con fluidez el inglés, tenía la "green card" e incluso podía pedir la ciudadanía. Pero se sentía muy solo, y estaba pensando que a lo mejor regresaba a México para casarse con alguna bella mujer y para trabajar en negocios de turismo. La profesión de coyote, aquí, no era muy bien vista, y ya comenzaba a causarle problemas.

Les ofreció su casa, y la señora Martínez de Silveira aceptó porque, entre otras cosas, también estaba habituada a ofrecer hospedaje a toda la gente que pasaba por Ciudad de Guatemala, pero eso sí, puso una condición: la comida la prepararía ella, y contendría mucha cola de res que es buena para

Lois Lane had just died, and Clark Kent didn't know what to do, weak and almost human before the inflexibility of destiny. In a Los Angeles movie theater, Doroteo and doña Asunción shared the same pained silence with their corpulent companion, Gabriel, the coyote who had aided them across the border and who had insisted on offering them refuge in his small house.

"No, please. Forget it. Keep your money," he had said to the old woman. "Others will pay, and, even better, you have to come and stay at my house in Los Angeles because there is no way that I am going to let you leave. Besides, you don't know how much you look like my grandmother, who is the one who raised me. She should be flying about right now, with the same white hair and the same hands as you, up there above in the heavens."

He was a bachelor, who weighed almost 250 pounds. He had been born in Guanajuato. As a small child he had lost his parents in an accident and, much later, upon the death of his grandmother, had left for the north to try out his luck. He had arrived fifteen years ago, and now he was thirty. He wasn't able to complain about his thirty years because he spoke English fluently, had his "green card", and could even apply for citizenship. But he felt very lonely. He was thinking that it would be better to return home to Mexico and get married to some beautiful woman and work in the tourism industry. The career of a coyote here was not viewed well, and it had already begun to cause him problems.

He offered them room and board, and Mrs. Martinez de Silveira accepted because, among other

componer la sangre, y ajo porque le habían dicho que era santo remedio contra toda clase de enfermedades e incluso contra la mala suerte.

La búsqueda del médico tuvo que esperar un par de días porque habían llegado el viernes por la noche, justo cuando se había terminado la semana de trabajo, de modo que madre e hijo se pasaron todo el sábado observando a Gabriel mientras armaba en el jardín un automóvil que era la mitad Ford y la mitad Volkswagen. El domingo, el carro funcionó, y en él habían salido de compras y, ahora, mientras caía la tarde, estaban viendo "Superman" en un cine del barrio.

El fornido coyote no pudo soportar la muerte de Luisa Lane y rompió a llorar sin consuelo. Aunque trataba de ser discreto, no podía soportar la desgracia irremisible que era capaz de tocar incluso a un personaje inmortal, y comenzó a gritar:

-Vuela, vuela. Anda, tienes que salvarla. Es la única forma.

Lo sabía porque ya había visto la película varias veces. Y lo decía con tanto dolor que posiblemente fue escuchado.

-Anda, tienes que salvarla.

Clark Kent, que hasta entonces no había sabido qué hacer, corrió hasta una cabina de teléfonos para despojarse de su ropa y convertirse en Superman. Antes de que pasara un minuto, alzó vuelo en forma vertical hasta llegar a la estratósfera, y, una vez allí, tomó aliento, todo el aliento que tan sólo puede tomar un hombre enamorado, y comenzó a volar en círculo en torno de la Tierra una, dos , tres y muchas veces hasta superar la velocidad de rotación del planeta; y

reasons, she was also used to offering her home to anyone who passed through Guatemala City. But she made one condition: she would prepare the food, which would include oxtail that was good for the blood, and garlic because they had told her that it was a holy remedy against every kind of sickness, including bad luck.

The search for a doctor had to wait a couple of days because they had arrived on a Friday night, just when the work week had ended. So, the mother and son spent all of Saturday watching Gabriel in the garden as he assembled an automobile that was half Ford and half Volkswagen. On Sunday the car worked, and in it they had gone shopping, and now, as night fell, they were watching "Superman" in the local theater.

The hefty coyote couldn't bear the death of Lois Lane and broke out crying inconsolably. Although he was trying to be discrete, he was not able to bear such an unpardonable misfortune that was capable of affecting even an immortal character, and he began to shout:

"Fly, fly! Go on, you have to save her! It's the only way."

He knew it because he had already seen the film several times. And he was saying it with so much grief that, probably, Superman heard him.

"Go on, you have to save her!"

Clark Kent, who until then had not known what to do, ran toward a telephone booth in order to shed his clothes and be transformed into Superman. Before a minute had passed, he took up flight until he arrived at the stratosphere, and, once there, he took a

voló tan veloz, con tanto amor y con tanta tristeza que también superó al tiempo, se le adelantó y pudo descender en picada cinco minutos antes de la muerte de Luisa lo que le pemitiría librarla, sana y salva, del peligro.

Cuando el hombre de acero y su novia, en suave descenso, se posaban sobre el tejado del Empire State Building tal vez pudieron escuchar los aplausos frenéticos de una ancianita de pelo plateado, un fornido coyote y un hombre calvo con la cabeza vendada. A partir de entonces, Manuel Doroteo Silveira Martínez viviría en Estados Unidos, mucho tiempo más de lo que el médico había predicho, y a veces fue muy feliz, pero raramente lo fue tanto como cuando Superman salvó a Luisa Lane. El día lunes y muchos días después, el carro de Gabriel daría vueltas y más vueltas alrededor de Los Angeles en busca del mejor médico de los Estados Unidos, pero no lo encontraron.

No es que no encontraran al mejor, sino que no llegaron a ver a ninguno. La primera vez que llegaron a un hospital, Gabriel hizo todo lo que pudo como traductor para explicarle a la recepcionista que estaban buscando al mejor médico de los Estados Unidos para que atendiera al señor calvo, "ése de la

deep breath, with the courage that only a man in love could have. He began to fly in a circle around the earth, one, two, three and many more times until he was able to surpass the velocity of the rotation of the planet; and he flew so rapidly, with so much love and with so much sadness, that he was able to transcend time.

He got ahead of it and was able to descend with a dive, five minutes before the death of Lois which allowed him to rescue her, safe and sound from the danger. When the man of steel and his girlfriend landed on the roof of the Empire State Building after a smooth descent, perhaps they could hear the frenzied applause of an old woman with silvery hair, a hefty coyote, and a bald man with a bandage over his forehead. From that point on, Manuel Doroteo Silveira Martinez would live in the United States, a lot more time much longer than what the doctor had predicted, and often he was very happy, but rarely was he so happy as when Superman saved Lois Lane. That Monday and many days later, Gabriel's car would go all throughout Los Angeles looking for the best doctor in the United States. But they did not find him.

venda, que está sentado allá al fondo, y esta señora es su madre que quiere ser la primera en hablar con el médico para que Doroteo no se entere porque da la casualidad de que él tiene un cáncer en el interior del cerebro, y el médico de Guatemala solamente le da tres semanas de vida, y eso si contamos a partir de hoy, y dice la señora que eso no es posible porque el señor es su hijo y siempre ha sido un hombre muy bueno."

"¿Cómo dijo? No, señorita. Comprenda que no le puedo hablar más fuerte porque no quiero que se entere ni por casualidad que la muerte lo anda buscando."

"Espere un instante, señorita, que la señora me está explicando algo más. Gracias por esperar, lo que la señora me dice es que quiere saber si los médicos de este hospital están aplicando ya un invento que ella leyó en "Selecciones" y que consiste en un agua muy clara que va pasando a través de todo el cuerpo sin que el hombre lo sepa y sin que sea de veras agua..."

...y aquella agua que no era agua era capaz de borrar la enfermedad, la desdicha, el fracaso, la adversidad, la desesperación, el miedo, la tristeza, el terror, el dolor, el sufrimiento, las lágrimas, la fatalidad, la rabia, la melancolía, la impotencia, el furor, la ansiedad...

..y aquella agua no pasaba por el cuerpo sino por la vida ...

...y se abría camino a través del destino y de la ilusión...

..y era capaz de curar la pesadilla, la duda, la decepción, la fatiga, la incertidumbre, el desencanto...

It's not that they didn't go to see the best, but that they didn't see anyone. The first time they arrived at a hospital, Gabriel did everything he could as a translator to explain to the receptionist that they were looking for the best doctor in the United States so that he might look at "the bald man".

"The one with the bandage... The one who is seated there at the back. And the woman is his mother who wants to be the first to speak with the doctor, so that Doroteo doesn't find out, because it so happens that he has cancer in his brain. And the Guatemalan doctor only gave him three weeks to live, and that is if we count today. And the woman says that this is not possible because the man is her son and he has always been a good man..."

"Wait just a second, miss. The woman is explaining something else to me..."

"Thank you for waiting, what the woman told me is that she wants to know if the doctors in this hospital are already making use of an invention that she read about in the Readers Digest and that consists of a very clear water that is passed through the whole body without the man knowing it, and without really being water..."

...and that water, that was not water, was capable of washing out sickness, unhappiness, failure, adversity, desperation, fear, sadness, terror, pain, suffering, tears, misfortune, anger, melancholy, impotence, rage, anxiety...

And that water didn't go through the body but through life, and a road was opened through destiny and illusion...and it was capable of curing nightmares, doubt, deception, weariness, uncertainty, disillusionment.

"Y déjeme explicarle, señorita, que esta señora cree haber leído en el mismo artículo pero no está segura de que fue allí de que las enfermedades terminales tienen origen en el alma, y no en el cuerpo, y por lo tanto el doctor no tendrá que trabajar mucho porque le bastará hacer algunos arreglos en el cuerpo..."

"¿Cómo dice, señorita? Un momentito, perdón, que ahora la traduzco. Mire usted, doña Asunción, la señorita quiere saber si hizo usted una cita con el doctor, si lo llamó o le escribió desde Guatemala."

"No, dice que no, pero que el doctor comprenderá cuando usted le cuente que Doroteo siempre fue un buen hijo."

"Y la señorita quiere saber también si ustedes tienen seguro, y qué clase de seguro tienen."

"La señora no sabe a qué se refiere usted."

"La señorita dice que en ese caso la primera consulta costará setecientos noventa dólares, más los impuestos, y además le pregunta si usted no tiene algún otro compromiso para el 19 de enero del próximo año a las diez y quince de la mañana. Caramba, eso es de aquí a siete meses, porque dice que para ese día puede programarle la cita."

"La señora pregunta si el doctor la podría recibir hoy mismo por la tarde. Dice, también, que por favor usted le pregunte si estaría dispuesto a aceptarle, en vez de los setecientos noventa dólares unas joyitas de oro que tiene, y éste que aquí le paso es su anillo de matrimonio. Levántelo para que sienta cuánto pesa."

"Señorita, por favor, no me interrumpa que solamente le estoy traduciendo lo que dice la señora."

"And allow me to explain to you, miss, that this woman believes, having read in the same article, but is not sure, that terminal sickness originates in the soul and not in the body. Therefore the doctor wouldn't have to work very hard because it would be enough to just put his body in order..."

"What did you say, miss? One moment, excuse me, now I will translate to her."

"Look, doña Asunción, the lady wanted to know if you had an appointment with the doctor, if you had called him, or written him from Guatemala."

"No, she said no, but that the doctor will understand when you tell him that Doroteo has always been a good son."

"And the lady wants to know as well if you have insurance and what kind of insurance you have."

"The woman doesn't know what you are referring to."

"The lady says that in such a case the first consultation will cost seven-hundred ninety dollars, plus tax. Besides, she is asking if you don't have another commitment for the nineteenth of January of next year at 10:15 in the morning, goodness, that is seven months from now, because she says that on that day she can schedule you an appointment."

"The woman is asking if the doctor would be able to meet with her today, this afternoon. She also says to please ask him if he would arrange to accept, instead of the seven-hundred and ninety dollars, some pieces of gold jewelry that she has. And this here that she passed you is her wedding ring. Lift it so that you can feel how heavy it is."

"No, doña Asunción, parece que la gringuita no me escucha. Me da la impresión de que tiene algún problema en el oído e incluso parece que ni siquiera puede vernos. Ahora se ha ido y nos ha cerrado la ventanilla. Si usted quiere, esperamos a que abra otra vez."

Durante ciento cuatro días recorrieron setentisiete clínicas, hospitales y consultorios privados. Muchas veces prefirieron dejar al paciente en la casa para que no se incomodara mientras Gabriel y doña Asunción se lanzaban al vértigo de las autopistas en el extraño carro del coyote. Nunca, desde hacía muchos años, se había sentido tanto calor en Los Angeles, y tanto la ciudad como los edificios y los veloces carros parecían flotar sobre un vaho caliente de color naranja.

Así fueron esos días para ellos, pero las noches fueron diferentes: llegada a casa, la madre se revestía de un optimismo tan contagioso que se lo pasaba al coyote y al enfermo, y tal vez se lo hubiera comunicado a cualquier persona que estuviera hasta a veinticinco metros de ella. "Nada ocurre en la tierra que no provenga de la voluntad de Dios, y si este doctor no nos ha querido atender debe ser porque no es el mejor médico de los Estados Unidos, y Dios nos está cuidando para que lo encontremos uno de estos días."

"Y ese doctor hará que nunca más vuelvas a usar esa odiosa venda, y después de que todo esto haya pasado, si no te importa, Gabriel, nos iremos contigo a Guatemala y compraremos una gran finca de cultivo que tú administrarás, y de esa manera no tendremos que ir nunca a las ciudades porque es allí

"Lady, please don't interrupt me, I am only translating what the woman says."

"No, doña Asunción, it appears that the blond does not hear me. I have the impression that she has some problems with her ears and it appears as well that she can't see us either. Now she has gone and closed the little window on us. If you want, we can wait until she opens it again."

During one-hundred and fourteen working days they traveled to seventy seven clinics, hospitals, and private offices. Often they chose to leave the patient at the house, so he wouldn't be uncomfortable, while Gabriel and Doña Asunción threw themselves into the vertigo of the busy freeways in the coyote's unusual car. Never, since many years ago, had it been so hot in Los Angeles, and so hot that the city, like the buildings and the fast cars, appeared to float over a hot vapor of the color orange.

In this way, the days passed, though the nights were different: at the house the mother put on an optimism so contagious that it was passed on to the coyote and the patient, and it was felt by whomever was within twenty-five meters of her. "Nothing happened in this land that didn't come by the will of God, and if this doctor had not wanted to care for us, it was because he wasn't the best doctor in the U.S. God is watching us so we can find him one of these days. And that doctor will never make it so that Doroteo has to return to using that hateful bandage. Then, after all that will have taken place, if you don't mind, Gabriel, we will go with you to Guatemala. We will buy a big ranch that you will be in charge of, and in this way, we will never have to go to the city,

donde nos andan esperando el demonio y las enfermedades."

"En esos momentos, el enfermo tocaba una guitarra que el Angel Gabriel había comprado en Guadalajara, y a veces incluso reclamaba una copita de tequila para aclarar la garganta. Era como si en esa casa se acabara de inventar la alegría, y a la segunda copa, la voz de Doroteo se hacía tan intensa que era como si la muerte hubiera llegado a casa para emborracharse con él. Gabriel, por su parte, aseguraba que era buena idea la de irse a trabajar en el campo "porque lo que es aquí la vida ya no me está gustando, con esta gente de la "migra" pisándonos los talones, a uno ya no lo dejan trabajar honradamente." Y la conversación se repetía cada noche como si fuera un sueño que cada uno de los tres protagonistas debería soñar hasta el fin de los tiempos.

Y de esa manera, sin que lo advirtieran, Doroteo excedió largamente el tiempo que supuestamente le quedaba sobre la tierra, pero a su madre no le bastaba con eso: estaba dispuesta a lograr que se curara definitivamente y estaba segura de que lo lograría. Además, una noche tuvo un sueño en el que no había imágenes sino tan sólo la voz de un arcángel que le revelaba que el reino de Dios no estaba en los hospitales ni entre los médicos de Los Angeles. A la mañana siguiente, ella comenzó a hacer las maletas. Irían a la famosa universidad de Berkeley donde, según había leído, habían inventado una bomba atómica de un milímetro y medio de espesor que podía ser utilizada ventajosamente en la lucha contra el cáncer: era tan efectiva que al estallar en la mesa de

because that's where the demon and his sickness is waiting".

During that time, the sick man played a guitar that Gabriel had bought in Guadalajara, and sometimes he even drank a glass of tequila in order to clear his throat. It was as if in this house they had just invented happiness, and on the second glass the voice of Doroteo became so intense that it was as if Death had arrived at the house to get drunk with him. Gabriel thought that it was a good idea, to go to work in the country, because here life was no longer pleasing him, with border patrol stepping on his heels and not allowing him to work honestly. And the conversation was repeated each night as if it were a dream that each one of the three protagonists would be dreaming until the end of time.

In this manner, against what the doctor had predicted, Doroteo's life greatly exceeded the time that he was supposed to have left on this earth. It was not enough for his mother; she was ready to see that he was cured definitively and was sure that he would be. Besides that, one night she had a dream in which there were no images but only the voice of an archangel revealing to her that the Kingdom of God was not in the hospitals nor with the doctors of Los Angeles. The following morning, she began to pack. They would go to the famous university, in Berkeley, where according to what she had read, they had invented an atomic bomb, the size of a millimeter, and it could be utilized advantageously in the fight against cancer. It was so effective that upon explosion on the night stand of the patient, it vaporized the essence of the sickness and converted it into perfume.

noche del paciente, volatilizaba el humor de las enfermedades, y lo convertía en perfume.

A Berkeley no pudo acompañarlos Gabriel, pero los dejó en contacto con una familia peruana de apellido León: "Don Adriano y doña Gloria son buena gente: como su apellido lo indica. Siempre me han tratado como un hijo desde que nos conocimos en un mercado de las pulgas donde trabajamos juntos. Dígales que estoy bien, y que a ver si se animan a venir a quedarse un tiempo en mi casa. Dígales que sueñen conmigo. Dígales que a veces en sueños me veo visitarlos."

Los León eran los primeros peruanos que la señora Martínez de Silveira conocía, y le llamó la atención la manera tan graciosa como pronunciaban el castellano. "El canto puede variar de gente a gente pero se nota que todos somos la misma gente", se dijo después de que ellos fueran a recibirlos en el paradero del "Greyhound", y los llevaran hasta una casa en la que vivían junto con dos hijas solteras y un nieto pequeño. "La casa es chica, el corazón es lo que vale. Ustedes se quedan aquí hasta que don Doroteo se haya curado completamente, o hasta cuando ustedes quieran. No se preocupen por nada."

El otro peruano a quien doña Asunción conoció fue un escritor que trabajaba como profesor visitante

Gabriel could not accompany them to Berkeley, but he put them in contact with a Peruvian family of the last name León: "Don Adriano and doña Gloria are good people. They have always treated me like their son ever since we met at the flea market where we worked together. Tell them I am fine, and that I hope they will come and stay at my house for a while. Tell them to dream of me. Tell them that at times I see myself visiting them in my dreams."

The Leóns were the first Peruvian family that Mrs. Martinez de Silveira met, and the melodious way that they pronounced their Spanish caught her attention. "The song can vary from people to people, but you can tell that we're all the same people," she told herself when they went to meet them at the Greyhound bus stop, and they took them all the way to the house where they lived with two single daughters and a young grandson. "The house is small, but the heart is what really matters. You will stay here until don Doroteo has recovered completely, or until whenever you want. Don't worry about a thing."

The other Peruvian whom doña Asunción met was a writer who worked as a visiting professor at the university, and who had published books about witches and saints. She knew close to nothing about him, but she had heard that he wrote about the saints as if he knew them, and about real people as if he

en la universidad, y que había publicado libros sobre brujos y santos. Poco o nada sabía de él, pero escuchó que escribía sobre los santos como si hablara con ellos, y sobre las personas reales como si las estuviera soñando. No le pareció gran cosa.

Pero fue a buscarlo porque quería pedirle que la ayudara a conectarse con el sabio que, en esa universidad, había descubierto el remedio atómico contra el cáncer, y el peruano la escuchó con admiración, con los ojos fijos en ella, como si estuviera copiando su vida o como si los dos fueran personajes ficticios. Después, mientras la llevaba a pasear por el campus, le fue dejando caer, tratando de amortiguarla, la información que ella necesitaba. Y las noticias no eran precisamente buenas: Berkeley no tenía escuela de Medicina. Además, al parecer, todavía faltaba un poco para que se inventara la cura contra el cáncer. "¿Quiere decir usted que esta revista está equivocada? ¿Y, exactamente, como cuántos días faltan para que se cure el cáncer?"

El amigo peruano no lo sabía o tal vez no se lo quiso decir, y con respecto de la revista, no, no estaba equivocada. Lo que ocurría es que se trataba de un ejemplar de hacía treinta años. Allí se hablaba sobre las, entonces, futuras aplicaciones de la energía atómica en la medicina, y sobre los experimentos que durante esa época se hacían en los laboratorios atómicos de Lawrence, un anexo de la universidad de Berkeley.

Pero ella no se iba a dejar intimidar por aquel nuevo fracaso. Para entonces, madre e hijo ya estaban a punto de cumplir un año y un mes fuera de Guatemala, o sea que el enfermo había excedido en

were dreaming about them. She thought it was no big deal.

But she went to look for him because she wanted to ask him to help her get in touch with the wise man who, at the university, had discovered the atomic cure for cancer. The Peruvian listened to her with admiration, with his eyes fixed on her, as if he were copying her life or as if they were both fictitious characters. Later, while he took her for a tour of the campus, he began to disclose the information she needed at the same time trying to soften it. And the news wasn't particularly good: Berkeley had no school of medicine. And what was worse, the cure for cancer had not yet been discovered. "You mean to tell me that this magazine is wrong? And just exactly, how many days until they do find a cure for cancer?"

Her Peruvian friend didn't really know, or maybe he just didn't want to tell her, and regarding the magazine, no, it wasn't wrong. What was happening is that they were dealing with a magazine issue that was thirty years old. In it, they talked about what was then the future applications of atomic power in medicine, and about the experiments that during that time period were taking place in the atomic power laboratories of Lawrence, an annex to the university of Berkeley.

But she wasn't about to be intimidated by that new failure. About that time, it was a year and a month since they had left Guatemala, that is to say, Doroteo had outlived the doctor's prediction of remaining life by more than one year. That was good news, but it wasn't enough for doña Asunción. She had to obtain Doroteo's definitive cure, and she

un año el tiempo de vida que el doctor había predicho para él. Y sin embargo, empeñada en lograr la curación definitiva de Doroteo, doña Asunción de ninguna forma iba a regresarse a su país ahora como algunas veces su hijo se lo sugería.

Además, estaba claro que la muerte había sido burlada, pero no vencida. A todo esto, ¿cómo sería la muerte? Se la imaginó bella y triste, como dolida por algún amor imposible. Se le ocurrió que hacía la cosas contra su voluntad, y que llevarse a Doroteo no había salido de ella. Quizás la muerte permanecía en Guatemala o acaso estaría en ese momento, como antes ellos, tomándose fotos de tamaño pasaporte, haciendo colas interminables y buscando una visa en el consulado. O tal vez le habían negado la entrada a los Estados Unidos y ahora remontaba un cerro de arena y caminaba y caminaba para llegar cuanto antes.

Y, de todas maneras, la señora pensó que ya había conseguido algo . El escritor le había presentado por teléfono a una amiga suya, también peruana, que era trabajadora social en un hospital de la zona y que haría todo lo posible, y también lo imposible, para que Doroteo fuera visto por los médicos norteamericanos.

Y así fue. Lo que había tardado más de un año en buscar, Diana se lo consiguió en quince minutos. Trabajó un rato con la computadora de la oficina de admisiones, tecleó el nombre de Doroteo muchas veces y luego de algún suspenso, la impresora comenzó a lanzar un pequeño cartón.

-Este es el seguro de su hijo, y con él lo van a atender gratuitamente. La cita es para el lunes a las

wasn't about to go back to her country like as her son sometimes suggested.

Besides, it was clear that Death had been fooled, but not defeated. How might death be? She imagined her being beautiful and sad, like being hurt by an impossible love. She thought that perhaps Death did things against her own will, and that taking Doroteo was not her idea. Maybe Death remained in Guatemala or maybe she could be at that precise moment, as they had before, that she was having credit passport pictures taken, standing in endless long lines and looking for a visa at the consulate. Or maybe they had denied her entrance to the United States and she was climbing a sandy hill to arrive as soon as possible.

And, anyway, the old woman thought she had already gained something. The writer had introduced a friend of his to her by phone, also Peruvian. This woman was a social worker in a local hospital where she would do everything possible, and impossible, so that Doroteo could be seen by the North American doctors.

And that's how it happened. What had taken doña Asunción more than one year to find, Diana had obtained for her in fifteen minutes. She worked a little bit with the computer at the office of admissions. She keyed in Doroteo's name many times and after some suspense, the printer began to spit out a small piece of card stock.

"This is your son's insurance, and with it they will take care of him for free. The appointment is for Monday at ten thirty in the morning. Bring your son that day and make sure you arrive about a half hour

diez y media de la mañana. Traiga a su hijo ese día y lleguen una media hora antes. Por favor, no responda a ninguna pregunta que le hagan. En todo caso, venga a verme y no se preocupe más, porque yo los voy a acompañar todo el tiempo, seré su intérprete y hablaré por ustedes.

"Aunque no lo parezca, esta joven sabe hacia dónde camina" - se dijo doña Asunción mientras recibía el carnet y miraba a su interlocutora. Aquella tenía unos ojos tan intensamente oscuros que parecía que solamente había caminado de noche. Y serían precisamente aquellos ojos los que le dirían la dolorosa verdad. Fue luego de dos semanas de hospitalización y pasados muchos y muy prolongados exámenes.

"El doctor le dice que quizás Doroteo ya no tenga cura. Perdón, un momento... Sí, doctor, eso es lo que le estoy diciendo. Lo que ocurre es que el castellano es más sintético, y además la señora no necesita conocer esos detalles... El doctor está asombrado de que Doroteo pueda caminar en el estado en que se encuentra y quiere saber qué le ha estado dando, y qué médico lo ha estado viendo durante estos últimos meses... Sí, doctor, eso es lo que dice la señora, que le dio en la comida mucho ajo y cola de res... "

-Y dígale, Diana, que también le di sesos de vaca en forma de tortilla, pero dejé de dárselos porque todos los que comían sesos comenzaban a perder la memoria, o soñaban que la memoria los llevaba hacia una pradera verde e infinita...

"Perdone, señora, pero el doctor quiere saber si le ha estado dando alguna medicina... Sí, doctor, yerba buena, lo que la señora está respondiendo es que le

early. Please, don't answer any of the questions that they ask you. In any case, come see me and don't worry about anything else, because I will be with you the whole time, I will be your translator and I will speak for you."

"Although it may not seem like it, this young woman knows where she's headed"- doña Asunción told herself as she received her son's insurance card and gazed at her facilitator. She had intensely dark eyes which made it seem as though she had only walked by night. And it would be precisely those dark eyes that would tell her the painful truth. It came after the two weeks of hospitalization and many prolonged exams:

"The doctor says Doroteo may not have a cure. Excuse me, just a moment..."

" Yes, doctor, that is what I am telling her. Only that Spanish is more concise, and besides the Mrs. doesn't need to hear all those details..."

"The doctor is amazed that Doroteo can even walk, given the state that he is in and he wants to know what you have been giving him, and what doctor he has been seeing during these past few months..."

"Yes, doctor, that's what she says, that she gave him plenty of garlic and ox tail in his food..."

"Excuse me ma'am, but the doctor wants to know if you have been giving him some medicine..."

"Yes, doctor, mint, what the lady is saying is that she gave him mint in room temperature water and she would also tie it to his forehead to reduce the swelling... And she also says that they have not seen a doctor since they left Guatemala... And she wants to

dio yerba buena por agua del tiempo y que también se la ataba en la frente para bajarle la hinchazón.... Y dice además que no han visto a ningún médico desde que salieron de Guatemala... Y la señora quiere saber qué es lo que le ve de raro en su hijo... ¿Cómo dice, doctor? No, doctor, perdone pero eso no se lo puedo repetir. Recuerde que ella es una anciana."

Pero la anciana leyó en los ojos de Diana lo que aquélla pretendía ocultarle. Los análisis de sangre, los rayos equis, las sondas eléctricas, los ecos del ultrasonido se habían internado profundamente en el cerebro de Doroteo, pero no habían encontrado nada sano. Nada, la nada absoluta.

"¿Cómo dice, doctor? ¿Que ya no podrá seguir atendiéndolo? ¿Que puede, pero que de nada serviría? ¿Que a lo más le quedan tres o cuatro semanas de vida?

Nada, lo que se llama nada. Ya no había nada dentro de él. Si la enfermedad no avanzaba más, era porque no tenía más que destruir, y si la muerte no venía por lo quedaba de Doroteo, era porque, tal vez, engañada, se había pasado de largo. Lo asombroso era que este hombre seguía caminando, y lo hacía de la mano de su madre anciana, y caminaba ya sin sombra por en medio de un país que no era el suyo. Nada, no había materia viva en el interior de ese cuerpo, y lo que la ciencia demostraba era lo que cualquier persona sabe: que los hombres estamos hechos de esperanza y de barro, pero más de esperanza.

know what is so rare about her son... What was that, doctor?.. No, doctor, forgive me but I can't repeat that to her. Remember, she's an old lady."

But the old lady read in Diana's eyes what she was trying to hide from her. The blood tests, the x-rays, the electric catheters, the ultrasounds had been internalized deep inside Doroteos brain, but they hadn't found anything healthy. Nothing, absolutely nothing.

"What was that you said, doctor? You will not be able to keep seeing the patient? That you could, but it would be useless? That at most he has three or four weeks left of life?"

"The mother insists in asking what is wrong with her son."

"The doctor says it's nothing. "

Nothing, absolutely nothing.

And there was nothing inside him. If the sickness progressed no more, it was because it had nothing left to destroy, and if Death didn't come for the remains of Doroteo, it was because, maybe, fooled, she had gone by without noticing. The amazing thing was that this man kept on walking, and he did it with the help of his old mother, and in the middle of a country that wasn't theirs. Nothing, there wasn't a living thing inside that body, and what science could prove is what everyone already knew: that man is made of hope and clay, but more of hope.

Nada, pero nada. No había forma de rebelarse contra el destino. Esa fue la única vez en que la señora pareció demostrar que era un ser humano como otro cualquiera: apenas el doctor se hubo marchado, se desmayó y no volvió en sí sino después de varias horas.

Lo que se llama nada. A lo mejor todo era así. A lo mejor, las personas y las cosas no eran de verdad. A lo mejor, el mundo nunca había dado vueltas, y todo había sido una ilusión....

Pero allí estaba Diana, y también Marcelita León, para atenderla, y además el desmayo se había producido en una sala del hospital. A ella la vio otro médico, un tejano muy gordo que hablaba español y que reía como Papá Noel.

—La abuelita se va a poner bien. Por ahora estamos tratando de controlar su presión arterial. Lo que ha tenido es un ataque de hipertensión propio de su edad y de algún estado emocional. ¿Le dieron alguna mala noticia?

Pero,"¿habráse visto, Asunción?." ¿Ella, así como así, iba a dejarse vencer por una mala noticia?... "Las cosas que se ven en este mundo." Iba a tener que abrir los ojos pronto para que estas chicas tan bonitas no se continuaran preocupando. Pero los mantuvo cerrados porque quería seguir llamándose la atención por haber flaqueado en ese momento.

—No se preocupen— dijo el medico tejano, unas horas más tarde. Ya lo logramos. La señora ya está en su presión normal. Ahora debe estar durmiendo. Comprendan que es una viejita.

¿Una viejita, ella? Ya vería este gordo lo que le iba a decir cuando abriera los ojos. Pero, si ya estaba

Nothing, absolutely nothing. There was nothing inside her son. What we know as nothing. Maybe that was how everything was. Maybe people and things weren't real. Maybe the world had never turned, and everything had been an illusion. There was not other way to rebel against destiny. That was the only time that the woman seemed to show that she was a human being like any other. As soon as the doctor had left, she fainted and didn't come to until a few hours later.

But there were Diana and Marcelita León to help her out, and besides her fainting had happened in a hospital room. Now, another doctor came to see her, a plump Texan who spoke Spanish.

"Grandma is going to be okay. For now, we are trying to control her blood pressure. She's just had a hypertension episode proper for her age and her emotional state. Has she received some bad news?

But, had Asunción seen herself? Just like that, she was going to let herself be overwhelmed by a piece of bad news?... The things that we see in this world. She was going to have to open her eyes soon so that these beautiful girls could stop worrying.

"Don't worry ", said the Texan doctor, a few hours later. "We've made it. The woman now has her blood pressure back to normal. Now she must be sleeping. You have to understand, she's an old lady."

sana como decía el doctor, ¿para qué abrir los ojos? "Se ve cosas tan bonitas así, con los ojos cerrados."

-Cuando despierte, la vamos a dar de alta. Si tiene algún problema, llámenme a cualquier hora, y no se preocupen por nada. Soy el doctor Ramón de León. Pero eso sí, que descanse y que se cuide en la comida. Nada de sal, por supuesto.

¿Cuidarse en la comida?... Pero si era ella quien la preparaba, y los León estaban encantados con la cocina guatemalteca. No, señor, ya vería ese gordo facineroso del doctor lo que iba a decirle cuando despertara. Pero siguió descansando, los ojos cerrados, ·y extrañamente feliz. Quizás en ese momento estaba enterándose de algo que diría después y que había leído en alguna parte: que Dios está dentro de nosotros mismos más adentro de lo que nosotros estamos dentro de nosotros mismos.

"Pues sí. Eso. El problema es que creo que El mismo no lo sabe. Que si lo supiera, ya habría curado a mi muchacho. Pues no. Claro que no."

Despertó bien, y más segura que nunca de que los médicos se habían equivocado. Era una desilusión que también ocurriera eso en los Estados Unidos, pero en todo caso, su hijo no los había necesitado durante todo un año pues ninguno de aquellos horribles dolores de cabeza se había repetido. A lo mejor, el cambio de aires y la yerba buena habían sido su remedio. Pero, eso sí, ahora ya era bueno despedirse para evitar ser una carga.

An old lady, her? That fat doctor was going to get a piece of her mind when she opened her eyes. Yes, she was fine now, just like the doctor had said, why open her eyes? You can see such beautiful things like that, with your eyes closed.

"When she wakes up, we are going to discharge her. If she has any problem, call me whenever, and don't worry about anything. I am Doctor Ramon de Leon. But, please she should rest and watch what she eats. No salt, of course."

Watch what she eats? - But she was the one who prepared the food, and the Leons were happy with the Guatemalan cook. No, sir, that fat rascal of a doctor would see what she was going to say to him when he woke her. But she continued resting, eyes closed and amazingly happy. Perhaps, in that moment she was finding out something she had said in the future and had read someplace: that God is inside of ourselves deeper than we are inside of ourselves.

"But then. The problem is, I believe, God doesn't know it. Otherwise, He would have already healed my boy."

She awoke better and safer than the doctors had thought. It was a disillusionment that something like this would occur in the United States, but in any case, her son had not needed any doctor during the whole year and none of the horrible headaches had returned. At best, the change of air and the mint had been his remedy. But, now was a good time to say good-bye in order to avoid being a burden.

Leave the house? What did the old woman mean? Go where? But if it was okay here. . . No way! Doña

¿Irse de la casa? ¿Se imaginaba lo que estaba diciendo? ¿Irse hacia dónde? ...Pero si aquí estaba bien... No, de ninguna manera. Doña Gloria y don Adriano, Marcela y Pilar, las hijas que vivían en casa, y también los otros hijos que vivían cerca de allí: todos se opusieron a la pretensión de la abuelita. De ninguna manera permitirían que se fueran. Y por último, ellos no eran ninguna carga. Además de ayudar en la cocina, doña Asunción se pasaba el día cuidando de los once bebés de la familia. Sus padres pasaban un rato por la casa y los dejaban con ella todas las mañanas.

¿Y Doroteo? ¿Acaso no ayudaba en la compra de objetos para el mercado de las pulgas? Además, su formación de auxiliar de Contador le había permitido asesorar a la familia y a muchos inmigrantes amigos en la elaboración de la declaración de impuestos... De ninguna forma, ellos no representaban ninguna carga, e iban a tener que quedarse en la casa porque ya eran parte de la familia.

Así se fueron pasando, muy lentos, uno tras de otro, los meses en California: era como si el tiempo también se hubiera olvidado de correr, y por su parte la muerte no se atrevía siquiera a tocar la puerta de la casa sobre la que Marcelita había pegado una estampa de San Jorge derrotando al dragón. Los

Gloria and don Adriano, Marcela and Pilar, the little girls that were living in the house, and also the kids that were living near there: all were opposed to the pretension of the grandmother. No matter what, they were not allowed to leave. Anyhow, they were not a burden. Besides helping in the kitchen, doña Asunción spent the day caring for the babies of the family. Their parents left them with her every morning. And Doroteo? Wasn't he helping to shop for objects for the flea market? Besides, his training in helping accountants had permitted him to advise the family and many immigrant friends in the preparation of their tax returns. In no way at all were they being a burden, and they were going to have to remain in the house because they were already a part of the family.

That is how they were spending, very slowly, month after month in California. It was as if time had stopped running and Death had not dared to touch the door of the Leon's house, where Marcela had fastened a stamp of Saint George destroying the dragon. The only pathological symptoms that Doroteo had consisted of sudden attacks of stupor that lasted a few hours, but did not cause alarm. In

únicos síntomas patológicos de Doroteo consistían en repentinos ataques de estupor que le duraban varias horas, pero que no causaban alarma. En esos momentos, hablaba con los demás, pero no se escuchaba hablar, pensaba que no pensaba, soñaba que ya era difunto y circulaba por la casa con los ojos cerrados como si estuviera siendo guiado por su ángel de la guarda. -"Doroteo se ha ido a caminar un rato por los cielos"- decían. Cuando volvía en sí, era como si estuviera recuperando su cuerpo, como si se lo pusiera de nuevo: algo había en él que no era de este mundo.

Y doña Asunción cavilaba. Si los médicos del país más avanzado del mundo no podían curar a Doroteo, entonces la ciencia no servía para nada. Los hombres estaban viajando a las estrellas, pero no había un médico que curara, por ejemplo, el mal de ojos, la torcedura de espíritu ni el dolor de los amores imposibles, y no se sabía, ni siquiera de qué materia están hechos los sueños ni en qué lugar del cuerpo humano está situada el alma. Para nada. La ciencia no servía para nada. Si lo hubiera sabido antes, se habría quedado en Guatemala: un buen maestro curandero allí le habría quitado al muchacho ese terrible dolor de cabeza. ¿Pero, volverse, ahora? De ninguna manera. No aguantaría ese viaje el pobrecito. Un momento... ¿no habría acá curanderos como aquellos que allá en Guatemala llamaban arjunes y que nacían con una raya cruzada sobre la frente en forma de cruz?

No, arjunes, no. Pero de los otros, sí los había y eran muchos. Pilar León había oído hablar de un maestro ecuatoriano que tenía su consultorio en

those times, he was speaking with the others, but not listening to what he was saying, thinking that he was not thinking, dreaming that he was already a corpse, and going around the house with his eyes closed as if he was being guided by a guardian angel. "Doroteo has been walking through the sky for a while," they said. When he came to himself, it was as if he was recovering his body and putting in on again: something was in him that was not of this world.

And doña Asuncion reflected. If the doctors of the most advanced country of the world could not cure Doroteo, then science served for nothing. Men were traveling to the stars, but there was not a doctor that could cure, for example, eye disease, spirit twisting, or the pain of impossible love. And it is not known, not even in what place of the human body that the spirit, the dreams, the dark shadows, or fate are located. For nothing! Science is useless. If she had known that before, she would have stayed in Guatemala. A good master healer would have gotten rid of that terrible headache. But, go back now? No way. The poor guy would not be able to endure that trip. Hold on . . . Wouldn't there be healers here like the ones in Guatemala called arjunes who were born with two stripes over the forehead in the shape of a cross?

No, arjunes, no. But of the others, there were, and there were a lot. Pilar Leon had heard them speak of an Ecuadorian master who had his office in the Mission District, of San Francisco where many Hispanics live. Of course, Pilar offered to accompany her. No, it was not necessary that Doroteo go with them. It was enough to bring one's own stuff: perhaps

Mission, un barrio de San Francisco donde viven muchos hispanos, y por supuesto se ofreció a acompañarla. No, no era necesario que Doroteo fuera con ellas. Bastaba con llevar una prenda suya: tal vez, un pañuelo. ¿Cuándo la llevaría? Ahora ya era viernes por la tarde. El próximo lunes, con toda seguridad, irían juntas a Mission.

¿Esperar hasta el lunes? "No, hijita, no estamos para darle tiempo al tiempo. Ese hombre va a curar a Doroteo, como que me llamo Asunción." La convenció, y partieron. Dos horas más tarde, después de haber cruzado el Bay Bridge a más de la velocidad tolerada y de haberse perdido largo rato en calles sospechosas, arribaron al tercer piso de un hotelucho infame y lograron entrevistarse con don Manuelito, el maestro ecuatoriano.

-Pero, qué lástima,no.- Les explicó que no iba a poder atenderlas ese día porque lamentablemente habían llegado tarde.

-La señora viene desde Guatemala, y tiene a su hijo muy malito. Ande, don Manuelito, no se fije tanto en la hora. Ni que fuera gringo.

No, no se trataba de eso. Si por él fuera... Si por él fuera, pero tenía órdenes muy estrictas. Ordenes de arriba.

En cambio, el lunes sí. Ese día tendrían prioridad sobre los otros pacientes, y ni siquiera tendrían que pagar por la consulta.

¿Pero qué órdenes de arriba podían ser tan poderosas para no atenderlas ahora mismo?

Se lo reveló. Don Manuelito curaba a sus enfermos asesorado por un tres médicos difuntos que examinaban al paciente y deliberaban en el cielo.

a handkerchief. When would they go? It was already Friday afternoon. Next Monday, with all certainty, they would go there together.

Wait until Monday? "No, honey, we can't lose any time. That man is going to cure Doroteo, just as my name is Asuncion". She convinced her, and they parted. Two hours later, after having crossed the Bay Bridge at a faster than tolerated speed and losing time in suspicious streets, they went up to the third floor of an infamous, run-down hotel. They succeeded in interviewing with don Manuel, the Ecuadorian master.

But, what a pity, no. Not that day, nor that hour. He could not attend to them. Not that day because, regretfully they had arrived late.

"The woman comes from Guatemala and has a very sick son. Go on, don Manuel, don't pay so much attention to the time as if you were a gringo."

No, it did not have anything to do with that. If it were up to him... If it were up to him, but he had strict orders. Orders from above...

But Monday, yes. That day they would have priorities over the other patients, and they would not even have to pay for the visit.

What orders from above can be so powerful that he does not attend them now?

He revealed it to them. Don Manuel healed his patients with the advice of three dead doctors who deliberated in the sky.

"What time does your watch say?"- he said- "A quarter after five, right? Like mine. I am sorry but what happens is they close the office for consultation at five."

-¿Qué hora tiene usted en su reloj? Las cinco y cuarto, ¿no? Como en el mío. Lo que pasa es que ellos atienden nomás hasta las cinco. A estas horas ya han cerrado su consultorio.

Claro que esperarían hasta el lunes.

-No te preocupes tanto,Pilarcita.- le rogó doña Asunción y le aseguró que pensándolo bien, no había tanto apuro porque Doroteo ya estaba recuperándose. Su único problema era que se escapaba del mundo por minutos.

Pero no sabía que le esperaba una sorpresa. Doña Asunción había cumplido 79 años en Los Angeles y llegaría a los 80 en Berkeley. Al llegar a casa, luego de la fallida visita al curandero, se encontró con una fiesta que los León habían organizado en su honor y que habría de congregar un poco más de ochenta personas

En la reunión, la señora se encontró nuevamente con el catedrático peruano y le aconsejó que se protegiera contra el mal de sombras, una enfermedad que atacaba a los escritores, y que consistía en sufrir un repentino ataque de pánico en los caminos, resultado de entrar y salir con demasiada prisa del mundo de sus criaturas.

A veces a uno podía partírsele la sombra. Fueron interrumpidos por un cantante argentino que se hacía llamar el "chansonier de las Américas". "Sombrita, vuélvete pronto. Vuelve que te voy a extrañar".-

Of course they would have to wait until Monday.

"Don't worry so much, Pilar," begged doña Asunción. She assured her that thinking well, she was not in a hurry because Doroteo was already recuperating. His only problem was escaping our world for minutes at a time.

But she did not know that she was waiting for a surprise. Doña Asunción had turned 79 in Los Angeles and would turn 80 in Berkeley. Upon arriving at the house, after the unsuccessful visit with the healer, she encountered a party with a little more than eighty people that the Leons had organized in her honor.

In the gathering, the old woman was found with the Peruvian professor and she advised him that he should protect himself against the sickness of shadows, an illness that attacks writers, and consists of suffering sudden attacks of panic on the highway. It was the result of entering and leaving too quickly the world of their creations. At times one could tear himself away from the shadow. They were interrupted by an Argentine singer who called himself the "Chansonnier of the Americas." "Little shadow, return soon. Come back because I'm going to miss you," he was singing with a voice that had been designed and modulated so that it would assume the smell and flavor of a far off distance.

"When people speak of the shadow, they speak of nagual. One that thinks about shadows does so because he goes about missing his nagual," doña Asunción suddenly said. The professor did not want to ask her what a nagual was because he realized that

cantaba con una voz que había diseñado y modulado para que aparentara el olor y el sabor de una insalvable distancia.

-Cuando la gente habla de la sombra, habla del nágual. El que piensa en sombras lo hace porque anda extrañando a su nágual- dijo de pronto doña Asunción, y su interlocutor no quiso preguntarle qué era un nágual porque se dio cuenta de que ella estaba hablando consigo misma, con su alma, como hablan las mujeres cuando están planchando.

-¿Cómo que no sabe lo que es un nágual? Es un pedazo de la sombra. Es un pedazo de nuestra sombra. Es un pedazo de nuestra sombra que se nos ha escapado.

Cualquiera podía darse cuenta que la señora estaba hablándose y probablemente convenciéndose a sí misma. Hablaba como si de pronto hubiera encontrado algo perdido:

-Le explicaré mejor para que usted me comprenda: el mismo día y a la misma hora en que viene al mundo un hombre, nace en el bosque un animalito que será su doble, y desde ese momento, la vida de uno y la del otro quedan atadas para siempre. Ese animal es su nágual. Su salud y su destino están atados a él.

Y sí quería saber desde cuándo, también se lo contó: los hombres y las bestias estaban atados desde la época del pecado de Adán, y estarían así hasta el fin del mundo. Sí, claro, por supuesto, eso significaba que la salud de un hombre dependía de la de su nágual.

-¿En el Perú no le han enseñado eso? eso lo sabe cualquier niño en Guatemala. En fin... Ahora, quisiera

she was talking to herself, to her spirit, like women who are ironing talk to themselves.

"How does one know what a nagual is? It is a piece of the shadow. It is a piece of our shadow. It is a piece of our shadow that has escaped from us."

Any person could notice that she was talking to herself, and perhaps she was having a brilliant idea. She was talking as if she would soon find something she had lost. "I will explain to you so you can better understand me. The same day and same hour that a man enters the world, an animal is born in the forest that will be his double. And from that moment on, the life of one and the other is tied forever. That animal is his nagual. His health and his destiny are tied to him."

And if he wanted to know since when, she also told him. "Men and beasts were tied since the time of Adam's sin, and it will be so until the end of the world. Yes, of course, that signified that the health of a man depends on the health of his nagual.

"I am repeating it to you. . . . Now, would you like me to clear up any doubts? Do you know in what part of the United States could be found a forest so large, large enough that all species of animals of today and those that are extinct, that we see only in dreams, can live?"

The writer responded that, without a doubt, that place was Oregon, the state north of California. He added that, according to a scientific report, each spring trees appear that still have not been dreamt.

"Then that is the place I'm looking for. There my son will be cured. It will be enough when we find his nagual... "

que usted me despeje una duda. ¿Sabe usted en qué parte de los Estados Unidos podría hallar un bosque tan grande pero tan grande que puedan vivir en él todas las especies animales de hoy y también las que no existen ahora, pero que ya estamos viendo en sueños?

El escritor le respondió que, sin lugar a dudas, ese lugar era Oregon, el estado que se encuentra al norte de California, y añadió que, según un informe científico, cada primavera, aparecían allí árboles que todavía no habían sido soñados.

-Entonces, ése es lugar que estoy buscando. Allá podrá curarse mi hijo. Bastará con que encontremos a su nágual...

Pero ella no iba a poder seguir pensando en un nuevo viaje ni en un tipo diferente de curación. No por el momento porque inmediatamente después de la fiesta, el sábado, la desdicha anunciada por los médicos comenzó. Luego de tres sucesivos ataques espasmódicos, Doroteo había caído en un letargo tan profundo que no había forma de despertarlo. No respondió a los llamados de su madre para que tomara la sopa, ni al olor del agua florida que le acercaron para que oliera ni a las gotas de agua bendita que dejaron caer sobre su frente. A las seis de la tarde, llegó el doctor. Era Ramón de León, el simpático gordo tejano que reía como Papá Noel.

Pero esta vez estaba siencioso y reservado. Luego de auscultar al paciente con mucho detenimiento como si estuviera atendiendo a un niño, se encaró con doña Asunción: ya no era necesario ni siquiera hacerle exámenes de laboratorio. Ahora estaba claro que Doroteo estaba muriendo dulcemente.

But she was not going to be able to continue thinking about a new trip or about a different type of cure. Not for the moment, because on Saturday the misery announced by the doctors began. After three successive spasmodic attacks, Doroteo had fallen into a lethargy so profound that it was impossible to wake him. He did not respond to his mother's calls to eat the soup, or to the smell of the flowery water that was brought close to him so that he would smell it, or the drops of the blessed water that they dropped over his forehead. At six in the evening, the doctor arrived. It was Ramon de Leon, the nice round Texan that laughed like Santa Claus.

But this time he was silent and reserved. After meticulously examining the patient as if he were attending a child, he spoke face to face with doña Asunción. It was not necessary, not even to do laboratory tests. Now it was clear that Doroteo was gently dying.

"He has lasted more than a year since they diagnosed his illness. He has not had pains during all that time. That, sincerely, ma'am, is a miracle. Now he is not going to suffer because from one moment to another he is going to meet with dreams of death.

-Ha durado más de un año desde que le pronosticaron el fin. No ha tenido dolores durante todo ese tiempo. Eso, sinceramente, señora, es un milagro. Ahora tampoco va a sufrir porque de un momento a otro va a encontrarse en sueños con la muerte.

¿Cuánto tiempo más iba a durar? Eso no lo sabía con precisión. Ya había cesado el funcionamiento del cerebro. Ahora sólo faltaba que el corazón sufriera un colapso. Eso podría producirse en unas horas.

Instaló el suero intravenoso con muy poca convicción de que aquéllo sirviera para algo, y antes de marcharse: "Este hombre está agonizando y le quedan pocas horas de vida. Quizás tres. Horas más, horas menos, pero no llega al domingo" pronosticó.

Llamado por los León, un sacerdote llegó al rato. Era el padre Mark, Marquitos para sus feligreses hispanoparlantes, y tenía su parroquia en Independence, Oregon, pero se hallaba en Berkeley acudiendo a un cursillo de Teología de la Liberación. Impuso los Santos Oleos al durmiente y comenzó a rezar una oración, larga y triste, que se iba elevando como el humo, hacia un cielo muy alto. Allá arriba, seguramente los ángeles entonaban himnos de gloria, tocaban clarines y hacían sonar campanas mientras se aprestaban a esperar a Doroteo.

Cuando cesó el rezo, todo quedó en silencio y todos se miraron como si ya estuvieran muertos. Por su parte, Doroteo, tenía una sonrisa plácida y los párpados entrecerrados. Estaba, pero ya no estaba. Acaso ya había terminado de perder la sombra. Era evidente que ya había comenzado a habitar los dominios de la muerte.

"How much time does he have left? That I do not know with precision. The brain has already stopped functioning. What will happen next is a heart attack. That could be about within a few hours."

He set up the intravenous serum with little conviction that it was serving for something and before leaving he prognosticated: "This man is suffering and few hours of life remain. Perhaps three. Maybe more, maybe less, but he will not see Sunday."

Called by the Leons, a priest arrived later. He was Father Mark, Marquitos to his Spanish-speaking parishioners, and he had his parish in Independence, Oregon. He was in Berkeley responding to a seminar on the Theology of Liberation. He performed the Extreme Unction to the sleeper and began to pray a long and sad prayer that was elevating like smoke up to the very tall sky. Up there, the angels were harmonizing hymns of glory, playing clarions and ringing bells while they were preparing to wait for Doroteo.

When he stopped the prayer, all remained silent and everyone looked as if they were already dead. For his part, Doroteo had a peaceful smile and half-closed eyelids. He was, but he was not. Maybe he had already lost the shadow. It was evident that he had already begun to dwell in the domains of Death.

"We pray so that our brother Doroteo reaches the peace and the light of the blessed ones very soon."

"Not too soon, Father," thought the well-educated Asuncion although she did not voice it. "And the well-educated woman who I am, I did not ask him how is possible that today's priests don't believe in miracles." When the priest and the doctor were about

-Recemos para que nuestro hermano Doroteo alcance la paz y la luz de los bienaventurados muy pronto.

"No tan pronto. No vaya tan rápido, padre".-lo pensó, pero no lo dijo, de puro bien educada doña Asunción. "Y de puro bien educada no le pregunté que cómo era posible que los sacerdotes de hoy no creyeran en los milagros." Cuando el sacerdote y el médico se hubieron marchado, anunció sus propósitos a la familia con un tono que no dejaba lugar a réplica: definitivamente, no confiaba en el diagnóstico del médico tejano y, en cuanto a lo dicho por el Padre Mark, ella rezaría, sí, pero de ninguna forma iba a pedir que aceptaran a su hijo ahora mismo en el cielo.

Todavía no era el momento. Ahora iba a rezar a Dios para implorarle que de una vez por todas curara al muchacho, y que corrigiera a tiempo la grave injusticia que iba a cometer llevándose prematuramente a un hombre que siempre había sido un buen hijo y un cristiano excelente.

Gloria de León la acompañó en el rezo de un rosario de quince misterios, y después la dejó sola en su plática con Dios. Aquélla era una conversación en la que Dios no llevaba la mejor parte: doña Asunción le increpaba lo injusto que era y le hacía recordar lo gentil y noblecito que había sido Doroteo y lo lindo que se le había visto el día de su primera comunión cuando apenas tenía diez años. Y Dios no la dejaría mentir cuando ella decía que este joven había sido un ciudadano modelo y un esposo ejemplar, que había sufrido, como debió sufrir Nuestro Señor en el Monte de los Olivos, cuando su esposa murió en el trance

to leave, she announced her purposes to the family with a tone that did not allow room for an answer. Definitely, she did not trust the diagnosis of the Texan doctor or what said by Father Mark. She would pray, yes, but not that they would accept him in the sky now. His time was not now. Now she was going to pray to God to demand that once and for all He would cure the man, and that He would correct the grave injustice that He was going to commit by prematurely taking a man that always had been a good son and an excellent Christian.

Gloria de Leon accompanied her in the rosary prayer of fifteen mysteries, and after the prayer she left her alone in her conversation with God. That was a conversation in which God did not carry the better part. Doña Asuncion scolded Him for the injustice and reminded Him how gentle and noble Doroteo had been and the beauty that he had seen the day of his first Communion when he was barely ten years old. And God would not stop her from lying when she said that the young man had been a model citizen and an exemplary husband, who had suffered, like Jesus suffered on the Mount of Olives, when his wife died in labor and there lost the long-awaited for son and the love of his life. He never married again because he wanted to keep her permanently in his happy memories. During all of his adulthood he had been the support of his aging mother and the example of all his family. Was it fair that He would take him anyway? No, God, it seems that you were wrong here.

del parto, y que no se había vuelto a casar porque quería permanecer fiel a ese recuerdo, y había sido durante toda su madurez el sostén de su madre anciana y el ejemplo de toda su familia. ¿Era justo que así como así se lo llevara? "No, Diosito, parece que aquí sí te equivocaste."

Quienes comenzaron a equivocarse fueron el médico, la ciencia y la propia naturaleza porque el hombre, clínicamente muerto, sobrevivió al sábado y llegó al domingo, y también a la tarde del domingo al lado de una madre que había pasado de increpar a Dios a darle buenos consejos como si también fuera su hijo. Al final, cuando llegó el lunes, Doroteo seguía viviendo, lo que ya era un prodigio, aunque doña Asunción lo sintiera completamente normal, como el alba o la luz, como el amor o los árboles, como son de normales los milagros.

Muy temprano, el lunes, le rogó a Pilar León que la llevara a ver a don Manuelito: "Tenemos una cita para ahora, no te olvides, y por mi Doroteo no te aflijas. A él lo cuida Dios, y allí estará esperándonos hasta la vuelta. Y vamos ya que no quiero llegar tarde a la consulta otra vez".

Llegaron a la hora, y fueron recibidas de manera muy cariñosa por el maestro quien se puso de inmediato a auscultar el pañuelo que le habían llevado, y con el cual habían secado la cara del enfermo.

Contuvo en la boca un sorbo de agua florida, y luego lo escupió sobre la tela, pero nada extraordinario ocurrió. Entonces repitió la operación mientras rezaba entre dientes una oración secreta, y sin embargo el pañuelo continuó siendo pañuelo, y

Those who were mistaken were the doctors, science, and nature itself because the man, clinically dead, survived Saturday and made it to Sunday, and also to Sunday afternoon at the side of a mother who had scolded God by giving Him good advice as if He were her son. When Monday arrived, Doroteo lived, which was a miracle, although doña Asuncion was feeling completely normal, as normal as miracles are, like the dawn or the light, or love, or trees.

By Monday morning, she begged Pilar Leon to take her to see don Manuel: "We have an appointment for now, don't forget, and for my Doroteo don't grieve. God is taking care of him, and he will be waiting for us there until we return. Let's go. I don't want to be late for the appointment again."

They arrived on time and were received in a very caring manner by the master who immediately began to examine on the handkerchief that they had brought. It was that handkerchief that had dried the face of the sick man.

"No, this is not possible. No way. This man is not here. I'm sorry but he is not here, in this life."

But he did not keep the diagnosis: he had to confirm it with the opinion of the three dead doctors. They told him "no. " Unfortunately, there was

nada quizás cambió en el universo. Entonces, muy preocupado, puso el oído sobre el pañuelo y sólo atinó a escuchar una vieja canción ranchera que se había perdido en el otro mundo. Pero no olió ni vio el alma de Doroteo.

-No, esto no es posible. No, de ninguna manera. Este hombre ya no está aquí. Lo siento, pero ya no está en esta vida.

No se conformó con su propio diagnóstico: tenía que confirmarlo con la opinión de los médicos invisibles. Los llamó con urgencia, pero aquéllos no acudieron.

Cuando al fin pudo ubicarlos, cerca del Purgatorio, le dijeron que desgraciadamente ya nada podía hacerse, y cuando don Manuelito insistió, ellos, dale con que ya no podían hacer nada, le dijeron que no, que ya habían visto al espíritu de Doroteo dando vueltas por diversos lugares del cielo.

De regreso a casa, doña Asunción le explicó a Pilar la causa por la cual creía que, incluso, aquel diagnóstico sobrenatural también estaba equivocado.

-Aunque estén el otro mundo, no dejan de ser médicos.

Y cuando llegaron, por cierto que Doroteo seguía viviendo. Y también al día siguiente y en los días que completaban la semana. Aquéllo convenció a los León que los milagros eran algo más cotidiano de lo que antes habían supuesto, y se entregaron por completo a la tarea de apoyar a la anciana con la seguridad de que Dios atendía las veinticuatro horas, solía hacer la siesta en las casas de los pobres y era capaz de aceptar, sin ofenderse, las críticas y los reproches de una madre anciana.

nothing they could do for Doroteo. Besides they had already seen the spirit of the Guatemalan flying through some places in the sky.

On returning home, doña Asuncion explained to Pilar the cause for her believing that supernatural diagnosis was also wrong.

"Even if they are in another world, they don't stop being doctors."

When they arrived, Doroteo was still alive. And also the following day and the rest of the days of the week. That convinced the Leons that miracles were something more common that they had earlier believed. They completely surrendered to the work of the old woman with the security that God is listening to His people twenty four hours, being accustomed to napping in the houses of the poor and being capable of accepting, without offending, the critiques and the reproaches of an ancient mother.

In the days that followed, the mother passed through Berkeley, Oakland, San Francisco, and practically the whole Bay Area accompanied by some of the family members, at times by Diana, the "Chansonnier of the Americas," the sceptic Texan doctor or whichever of the friends that she had known in the Leon house. One after another, healers, parapsychologists, reciters of prayers, lamas, witches, naturopaths, acupuncturists, chiropractors, spiritualists, homeopaths, yogis, and herbalists visited with the security that in any moment they would find the remedy. Meanwhile, the state of the patient remained the same in a coma portentous as well as infinite.

En los días que siguieron, doña Asunción recorrió Berkeley, Oakland, San Francisco y prácticamente toda el área de la Bahía acompañada por alguno de los miembros de la familia, a veces por Diana, el "chansonnier de las Americas", el escéptico médico tejano o cualquiera de los amigos que había conocido en la casa de los León. Uno tras de otro, visitaron curanderos, parapsicólogos, rezadores, lamas, brujos, naturistas, acupunturistas, quiroprácticos, espiritistas, homeópatas, yogas y herbolarios con la seguridad de que en algún momento encontrarían el remedio. Mientras tanto, el estado del enfermo permanecía estacionado en un coma tan portentoso como infinito.

Mariano y Josefina, "primeros mentalistas de prestigio mundial", recibieron la llamada de doña Asunción con más asombro que alegría porque no estaban acostumbrados a esa clase de clientes. Usualmente, tenían una hora de emisión en una radio en español, y allí leían cartas de supuestos clientes agradecidos por su capacidad para hacer frente a la envidia y solucionar problemas en el trabajo, para conjurar novias con mal aliento y apagar ensalmos de magia negra o para ubicar y devolver esposas fugitivas y objetos robados, y por lo tanto, sus clientes eran jóvenes "hispanas" suspirantes, parejas mal avenidas o comerciantes con mucho dinero y poca suerte, o al revés, pero no precisamente una anciana empecinada en mantener vivo a su hijo. No la hubieran recibido jamás si no hubiera sido porque su voz se metió en el aire en la hora de mayor sintonía.

"¿Cómo dijo que se llama? ¿Asunción? ¿Dijo usted que se llamaba Asunción? ...Asunción, qué hermoso nombre! ¿Y de dónde se reporta?... Señoras

Mariano and Josefina, the "First World Renowned Parapsychologists " received the call from doña Asuncion with more amazement than happiness because they were not accustomed to that class of clients. Usually, they had one hour of broadcast on a Spanish radio station, and there they read letters of supposedly grateful clients by their capacity for confronting jealous friends, work problems, helping girlfriends with bad breath, and black magic spells or locating fugitive wives, or stolen objects, and therefore their clients were young, sighing Hispanic young women, irreconcilable couples or merchants with a lot of money and little luck or the reverse, but not precisely a stubborn, old woman who was trying to keep her son alive. They would have never received her but her voice interfered during their most popular hour.

"What do you say your name is? Asunción? You said you are called Asuncion? ... Asuncion, what a beautiful name! And from where are you calling?... Ladies and Gentlemen, she is calling from Berkeley, California. Nothing less than from Berkeley, California, through the waves of ether, to the studio of your friendly radio in Oregon. And what can I help you with, ma'am?

"What did you say? Can we remove a coma from a man that has always been respectful to his parents and is in a coma but hasn't dye because of a miracle from Heaven?... Is this a joke? Listen, Josefina, this is not one of the recordings that we have prepared."

"Be quiet, we are on the air... Hurry, put on the musical screen."

(Sound of the gong. Chords of the Fifth Symphony).

y señores, nos están llamando desde Berkeley, California. Nada menos que desde Berkeley, California, por las ondas del éter, hasta el estudio de su radio amiga, en Oregon. ¿Y en qué se la puede servir, señora?"

"¿Cómo dijo? ¿Que si podemos sacar del coma a un joven que siempre ha sido respetuoso con sus padres y que permanece en coma sin morirse debido a un milagro de la Virgen?...¿Esto es una broma? Oye, Josefina, ésta no es ninguna de las grabaciones que teníamos preparadas..."

"Cállate, que estamos saliendo al aire... Pronto, mete la cortina musical".

(Sonido de gong. Acordes de la Quinta Sinfonía).

Por el teléfono interno, en confidencia y fuera de la emisión, hablaron con doña Asunción, y ella les explicó su problema, pero los primeros mentalistas de prestigio mundial no tuvieron alma para engañarla, y se limitaron a decirle que le enviarían por correo una copia del Cristo Afortunado y otra del Escapulario de los Tres Deseos, milagrosísimas reliquias que ellos acababan de traer de Tierra Santa, y de las que justamente ahora estaban haciendo una promoción a través de las ondas de su radio amiga.

Pero no cesó allí la búsqueda del remedio. "Ya estoy vieja. No me queda mucho tiempo para cansarme ni para deprimirme". El chansonier de las Américas la llevó a ver a un grupo religioso oriental cuyos miembros curaban de una manera prodigiosa. Mantenían las palmas de la mano a menos de un metro del paciente al tiempo que recitaban oraciones en japonés antiguo. El servicio era gratuito y la mayoría de los practicantes eran "hispanos"

Through the internal telephone, in confidence and outside of the broadcast, they spoke with doña Asunción. She explained her problem to them, but the first mentalists of the renowned world did not have the spirit to deceive her. They limited themselves to telling her that they would send to her through the mail a copy of the Lucky Christ and another of the Scapular of the Three Wishes, miraculous relics that they had just brought from Holy Land, and they were on sale.

But she did not stop her search for the remedy there. "I am already old. It doesn't leave me much time to be weary or depressed." The Chansonnier of the Americas took her to see a religious, Oriental group whose members cured in a prodigious manner. They kept the palms of their hands at least one meter from the patient at the time that they were reciting prayers in ancient Japanese. The service was free and the majority of the practitioners were Hispanic volunteers who could pray without stopping a prayer that lasted two hours and that they did not understand. And, finally, the temple that they practiced in was a pagoda that had been brought through the sky from Japan to San Francisco.

They could not cure the patient, but they found out the explanation to his illness, an explanation that was sincere: in a street in Guatemala, Doroteo had been eating an apple one day. Instead of keeping the core so that he could put it in the garbage, he threw it into a garden. There, it had fallen over the head of a goblin, famous for its bad temper and for being very careful of good manners. In those moments, Doroteo should have recited a prayer in ancient Japanese, but

voluntarios que podían rezar sin cansarse una oración que duraba dos horas y que ellos no comprendían. Y, por último, el templo en el que curaban era una pagoda que había sido traída por los cielos desde el Japón hasta San Francisco.

No pudieron curar al paciente, pero encontraron la explicación de sus males, la cual era sencilla: en una calle de Guatemala, un día Doroteo había estado comiendo una manzana. Cuando sólo le quedó el centro, en vez de guardarlo para llevarlo a un depósito de basura, lo tiró sobre un jardín. Allí había caído sobre la cabeza de un duende famoso por su mal genio y por ser muy cuidadoso de las buenas maneras. Lo que, en esos momentos, debería haber hecho Doroteo era recitar una oración en japonés antiguo, pero no se sabía ninguna, y el duende enfurecido se metió dentro de su cabeza. Ahora ya había pasado mucho tiempo y había desaparecido la posibilidad de salvarlo. El problema, sencillo al principio, se había tornado insoluble. Ni más ni menos de la forma como una gripe mal curada puede convertirse en tuberculosis.

Diana conocía otro lugar de curaciones prodigiosas: el Centro Taoísta. Antes de ir allí, ella solía tomar vitamina B para no pelearse con su enamorado. Ahora, gracias a la ciencia del Tao, ya no era necesario... Las atendió el maestro Si Fu, un venerable anciano oriental cuyo método de diagnóstico era la toma del pulso. Asía de la muñeca al paciente, pero en vez de contar los latidos, trataba de ver si hacían música: como sobre un piano, iba tocando: Do, re, mi, fa, sol, la, si. Si, la, sol, fa, mi, re, do. En caso positivo, si los latidos eran rítmicos, la

he did not know any. The goblin, enraged, interfered inside of Doroteo's head. Now, much time had already passed, and the possibility of saving him had disappeared. The problem, minor from the start, had turned insoluble. Like a poorly doctored cold can be turned into tuberculosis.

Diana knew another place of prodigious cures: the Taoist Center. Before going there, she was used to taking Vitamin B so that she would not fight with her sweetheart... The master Si Fu, a venerable, old Oriental man, whose method of diagnosis was to check the pulse of the sick, assisted them. He took the wrist of the patient, but instead of counting the beats, he tried to see if they made music: like over a piano, he was playing do, re, mi, fa, so, la, ti. Ti, la, so, fa, mi, re, do. If they made harmony, the person was enjoying good health. If dissonant, the master needed to tune the patient.

But the veins of Doroteo were not giving the Yin nor the Yang. Long ago, the music had escaped his body. Desperate, the master applied the ear to the wrist, and he could only hear the notes of the piano very far away that were probably being played, in the heights, by an angel in the sky.

The sick one had spent fourteen days in a state of unconsciousness while his mother experienced the failure of a new hope every day. But that did not mean that she would stop helping him. Home for the night, she changed his serum and prayed with him as when he was a boy and used to ask her to repeat the prayers, even though he was in dreams. It was a long prayer that ended asking to God for the happiness of the poor, the sick, the ones who suffer injustices, the

persona gozaba de buena salud. De otra manera, el maestro tenía que afinar al paciente.

Pero las venas de Doroteo no daban el Yin ni el Yan: hacía tiempo, la música se había escapado de su cuerpo. Desesperado, el maestro aplicó el oído a la muñeca, y sólo pudo oír las notas de un piano muy lejano que probablemente estaba siendo tocado, en las alturas, por un ángel del cielo.

El enfermo había cumplido catorce días en estado de inconsciencia, mientras su madre transitaba cada día del fracaso a una nueva esperanza. Pero eso no significaba que dejara de atenderlo personalmente. De regreso a casa, por la noche, le cambiaba el suero y rezaba a su lado como cuando él era un niño, y le pedía que repitiera, aunque fuera en sueños, una larga oración que terminaba rogando a Dios por los pobres, por los enfermos, por los que sufren injusticias, por los que se han perdido en el mar. Y, por supuesto, también por los niños obedientes.

¿Faltaba alguien por visitar? "¿Nadie? ¿Cómo que nadie? ¿Y quién es la Dama Mágica del Caribe?"

-No, de ninguna manera. Eso jamás.- el Chansonier de las Américas se opuso terminantemente a esa visita, pero omitió las razones de su negativa. De hombre a hombre, le confió a don Adriano que se trataba de una venezolana cuyo verdadero nombre era Rosa Granadillo. Cantaba en un casino. Curaba del mal de arrugas, con aplicaciones de ginseng y miel de abeja. Conocía la ciencia de leer en la palma de la mano, y su poder era grande: tan grande como sus celos porque se pasaba la noche leyendo la mano de su esposo.

ones lost at sea, and of course, for the obedient children.

Was there someone left to visit? "No one? What do you mean no one? And who is the Dama Magica del Caribe?"

"No. Not at all. Never." - the Chansonier of the Americas was terminally opposed to that visit, but had omitted the reasons for his negative response. From man to man, he confided in don Adriano that it was about a Venezuelan woman whose real name was Rosa Granadillo. She sang at a casino. She removed wrinkles using ginseng and bee honey. She knew the science of reading palms, and her powers ' were great: as great as her jealousy because she spent the entire night reading her husband's palm.

And how did he know so much about her? "Very simple." They sang in the same Hispanic restaurants, and she was his fiercest competitor. But that was not the reason for opposing to see her. He did it because he did not find it proper that a lady like doña Asunción would interview herself with that Granadillo woman... More details: she made men delirious and she drove them to forgetfulness and craziness by merely singing in a very special note. The Chansonier spoke as he was not really speaking, he murmured for fear of being heard. But his eyes and his hands spoke, and doña Asunción listened.

"Where did you say she lived?... We will go see her immediately."

When they found her, the Dama Magica del Caribe was solving the problems of a Mexican who did not have his papers in order. "It's ready. Put this perfume on as you leave your house for work. If an

¿Y cómo sabía tanto acerca de ella?... "Muy sencillo." Cantaban en los mismos restaurantes hispanos, y ella era su más tenaz competidora. Pero ésa no era la razón para que se opusiera a que la vieran. Lo hacía porque no consideraba correcto que una dama como doña Asunción se entrevistara con la Granadillo... Más detalles: hacía delirar a los hombres, y los conducía al extravío y la locura con tan sólo cantar en una nota muy especial. El Chansonier habló como si no hablara, susurró, por temor de ser escuchado. Pero sus ojos y sus manos hablaron, y doña Asunción escuchó.

-¿Dónde dices que vive?... Iremos a verla inmediatamente.

Cuando la encontraron, la "Dama Mágica del Caribe" se hallaba solucionando el problema de un mexicano que no tenía los papeles en regla. "Ya está. Ponte este perfume al salir de tu casa hacia el trabajo. Si un envidioso te denuncia, se le caerá la lengua. Y los de la "migra" no te verán, y si te ven no podrán perseguirte porque de pronto los envolverá la música y comenzarán a bailar merengue."

Atendió a la anciana con cariño, pero ella tampoco podía ayudarla, y se lo dijo. Sus poderes alcanzaban para escuchar conversaciones que se estaban produciendo en otro lado del planeta o para ver a los barcos que habían zarpado del puerto hacía tres semanas, pero no servían para volver a encender un cirio que ya se había apagado en el otro mundo. Muerte y muerte, lo único que vio fue muerte.

-¿Y quién es esta Madame Divah? ¿Una adivina? ¿Es la última que falta? Vamos, pronto, a verla que no nos queda mucho tiempo.

envious man turns you in, his tongue will fall off. And those from the "migra" will not see you, and if they do see you, they will be no able to chase you down because at that moment the music will invade them and they will begin dancing merengue."

She attended the old woman with affection, but she also could not help her, and she told her. Her powers were enough to listen to conversations taking place at some other place on the planet, or to see boats that had lifted anchors from shore three weeks ago, but she was not good at lighting a candle that had been blown out in another world. Death and death. The only thing she saw was death.

Later, doña Asunción asked the Leons: "Who else could we see?... Why no one? And what about Madame Divah? Who is she? A fortune teller? Why not? Let's go, soon, to see her because not much time remains."

The woman shuffled the cards, separated the stack in two, and asked doña Asunción to uncover seven of them.

Bad cards. The King of Hearts was running away. The Princess of Clubs was dressed like a nurse. The Healing Queen winked an eye without saying yes or no. The Card of the Master did not have messages because the Master was very busy constructing the destiny of an unfortunate couple. The other three were the Lock, the Bolt, and Death cards.

She shuffled them again and nothing. There were no people or messages. It was as if time and the destiny of all the inhabitants of the planet had suddenly evaporated. In order to save the planet from a universal catastrophe, she changed decks, and

La mujer barajó las cartas, partió el mazo en dos y le pidió a doña Asunción que descubriera siete.

Malas cartas: el Rey de Copas se alejaba corriendo, la Princesa de Bastos estaba vestida de enfermera, la Reina Curandera guiñaba un ojo sin decir ni que sí ni que no, la Carta del Maestro no tenía mensajes porque el Maestro estaba muy ocupado reconstruyendo el destino de una pareja infortunada. Las otras tres cartas eran el Candado, la Tranca y la Muerte.

Barajó otra vez, y nada: no había personas ni mucho menos mensajes, era como si el tiempo y los destinos de todos los habitantes del planeta se hubieran evaporado de repente. Para salvar al planeta de una posible catástrofe universal, cambió de baraja, y lentamente volvieron a aparecer las cartas habladoras. Entonces, Madame Divah leyó en una carta la historia de miles de hombres, mujeres y niños que subían cerros, cruzaban la frontera, trabajaban como peones agrícolas y, después de muertos, se iban caminando debajo de la tierra para descansar en su patria del Sur. Y en otra carta, no había historia alguna sino una campana muerta cuyo sonido se desparramaba sobre la redondez de la tierra. Y en otra carta, había un grupo de mujeres caminando y caminando: "Es la carta de las madres ancianas. Como puede usted fijarse, tienen la mitad del alma en el Paraíso".

Que, por favor, ubicara pronto la carta de Doroteo. "¿Cuál dice usted que es?... ¿Esa? ...Pero, ésa no es un hombre".

slowly as she turned the cards, they began speaking in tongues.

Then, Madame Divah read in a card the story of thousands of men, women, and children that went up hills, crossed borders, worked as agricultural peons, and after dying, they walked under the land in order to rest in their native land of the South. And in another card, there had not been any story, but a phantom bell whose sound spread over the roundness of the land. In another card, there was a group of women walking and walking. Madame Divah said: "It is the card of the ancient mothers. As you can see they have half of the soul in Paradise."

"If you could please quickly locate the card of Doroteo.", the mother pleaded. "Which one do you say it is?... This one? But that is not a man."

No, it was not him. It was a woman with a long look and sweet eyes that for moments they were black, and at other times they were blue.

"Pretty, isn't she?" the card reader said. "But, you see, that lovely gringa is Death who goes searching for Doroteo."

No, no lo era. Era una mujer de mirada larga y de dulces ojos que por ratos eran negros y por largos momentos, azules.

-Bonita, ¿no? Pues, vea usted. Esa gringuita es la Muerte, y resulta que anda buscando a Doroteo.

Cuando se acabó la lista de curanderos mágicos, ya era el día trigésimo tercero del coma, y a la señora no le quedaba otra ocupación que permanecer en casa, cambiar el suero del paciente, mantenerlo aseado y fragante, y rogarle de vez en cuando que de una vez por todas despertara "porque lo que es, yo, hijito, ya estoy comenzando a preocuparme." Aquella misma tarde, recibieron una visita inesperada. Era nada menos que Gabriel, el ángel Gabriel como lo llamaban, el amigo de Los Angeles, el coyote que los había ayudado a entrar en los Estados Unidos, y en cuya casa habían sido tan felices.

-Ex-coyote. Si me hace el favor, abuelita.- corrigió el ángel Gabriel. Y le contó que muchas cosas habían cambiado en su vida desde el tiempo en que no se veían. En primer lugar, había cambiado de profesión: en vista de que tenía la facultad de resucitar carros viejos, se había dedicado a la mecánica. Había puesto un taller, y su negocio era próspero.

En segundo lugar: "Sorpresa: asómese a la ventana, y lo verá."

Lo que vio la señora no lo terminó de ver porque era una interminable casa rodante- compuesta de

When doña Asunción finished the list, it was already the thirty-third tragic day of the coma. The mother did not have anything left to do but stay home, to change the patient's catheter, to keep him clean and smelling good, and to beg him from time to time, once and for all, to wake "because whatever it is, my son, I'm starting to worry." That same afternoon, they received an unexpected visit. It was none other than Gabriel, the angel Gabriel as they called him, the friend from Los Angeles, the coyote who had helped them enter the United States, and in whose house they had been so happy.

"Ex-coyote. If you please, Grandmother," corrected the angel Gabriel. He told her that many things had changed in his life since the time that they had last seen each other. In the first place, he had changed his profession: in view of having the ability of fixing old cars, he had dedicated himself to the profession of auto mechanics. He had a workshop, and his business was prosperous.

"Secondly," he said "A surprise: lean out the window, and you will see it."

What the woman saw, she could not see the end of because it was a long motor home with five trailers behind that wrapped around the corner. It had been constructed, like the car he had built before, with the rest of the different cars and the different debris materials. From the window, they could see two and a half sleeper cars. Proudly, the ex-coyote added: "Do you know what is next?

The colors of the Mexican flag painted across the procession of trailers conferred upon them an exciting unity.

varios vagones- que daba la vuelta a la esquina y había sido construida, al igual que el vehículo anterior, con restos de carros diferentes y material de desecho. Desde la ventana hasta la esquina, podía verse dos y medio dormitorios. - "Y no sabe usted lo que viene después."

Los colores de la bandera mexicana pintados en ondas sobre cada vagón le conferían unidad al conjunto: "No. Usted no sabe lo que viene después."

Primero estaba la cabina del chofer y la sala. El otro vagón era el dormitorio principal y la cocina. Le seguía el vagón de huéspedes. "Los dos que vienen a continuación serán ocupados por usted y Doroteo. Porque ustedes se vienen a vivir con nosotros", anunció.

¿Nosotros? : Gabriel se había casado con una linda chica mexicana- "legal, sin problemas."

"Se llama Elisa, ¿sabe? ¿y sabe usted lo que significa llamarse Elisa?" - Elisa llegaría esa tarde por avión y estaba encantada "de saber que va a vivir con usted, porque, sabe usted, ella nunca conoció a su abuelita."

Ahora se estaban dirigiendo a Oregon.

"¿Dónde dices?"

"A Oregon, claro que a Oregon."

"¿Un país colmado de bosques?"

"Correcto. Allí mismo, allicito."

"¿Donde crecen árboles que nunca han sido soñados?"

"Pues la verdad que no lo sé. Pero sí, creo que sí"

"¿Y entre los árboles hay miles de náguales?"

"Pues mire que no lo sé. Pero si usted lo dice..."

First, it was the driver's cabin and living room. The next trailer was the principal bedroom and the kitchen. The next one was the host's trailer. "The two that are coming up will be occupied by you and Doroteo."- the angel Gabriel announced to doña Asunción.

More news: he had married a pretty Mexican girl- "legal, without problems"- Her name was Elisa and she would arrive that afternoon by plane and was charmed "to know she was going to live with you because, you know, she never knew her own grandmother."

Gabriel said: "We are right now going to Oregon."

"Where did you say? To Oregon?"

"To Oregon, of course to Oregon."

"A country overflowing with trees?"

"There, right there."

"The same Oregon where trees grow that have never been dreamed of?"

"Well, yes."

"And between the trees there are thousands of naguales?"

"Yes, no, well, I don't know."

He would start an excellent Christmas tree business, and was thinking to establish himself in a town called Independence where he would also dedicate himself to mechanics, and they had told him that there was an excellent university near there.

"They have told me that it is called Western, and at best, I'm going to have time to continue my education."

Hacía un tiempo, Gabriel había comenzado un excelente negocio de compra y venta de árboles de Navidad. Ahora viajaba al lugar donde crecían, y pensaba establecerse en un pueblo llamado Independence donde también se dedicaría a la mecánica, y le habían contado que cerca de allí había una universidad excelente.

-Me han dicho que se llama Western, y a lo mejor me doy tiempo para continuar estudiando.

Para lograr todo eso, iba a ser necesario e imprescindible que doña Asunción y Doroteo viajaran con ellos: "Ni Elisita ni yo vamos a podemos manejar una casa sin la experiencia de una persona como usted."

Y llegando nomás, los León le habían venido con la noticia de que Doroteo no se quería levantar de la cama. No, no le habían contado más. No habían tenido tiempo porque él había entrado corriendo a buscar a la abuelita. ¿Cómo que no se quería levantar? ¿Había salido de parranda la noche anterior? ¿Se había pasado de tragos? No, que don Doroteo, pero eso nos pasa a todos los hombres. No es para que usted se enoje, abuelita. ¿Cómo que no era cuestión de tragos? ¿Se estaba portando mal Doroteo? No, eso ni pensarlo.

Pero doña Asunción no respondió a ninguna de sus preguntas porque estaba transfigurada. De repente, preguntó:

-¿Estás realmente hablando de Oregon? ¿de los bosques de Oregon? ¿De Oregon Oregon?

-Pues sí. Le estoy hablando de Oregon Oregon, y si usted quiere Oregon Oregon Oregon.

In order to achieve that, it was going to be necessary and essential that doña Asunción and Doroteo travel with them. "Neither Elisa nor I will be able to manage a house without the experience of someone like you."

When Gabriel had arrived at the Leon's house, they had told him that Doroteo did not want to get up from the bed... No, they had not told him more... They did not have time because Gabriel had entered running to look for the grandmother.

"Why he doesn't want to get up? Has he spent the night reveling? Has he drunk too much? What a man, that don Doroteo" said Gabriel, "but all men do that. It is not to make you angry, Grandmother. Are you telling me that he wasn't drinking? Is he behaving badly? What's wrong with him?"

But doña Asunción did not respond to any of the questions because she was transfixed. Suddenly she asked:

"Are you really talking about Oregon? Of the forests of Oregon? Of Oregon Oregon?"

"Well, yes." He was talking about Oregon Oregon, "and if you want, Oregon Oregon Oregon. There are only trees and people there."- he continued.

There were only trees and people there. Dead and life ended there. Eternity began there: an eternity of pines and wild geese, eagles and cedars, swallows and sycamores, bears and falcons. From there, the salmons sailed toward Japan and then they came back to their home. The whales passed near the Oregonian coast singing a song to distant love. And then the eternity continued: another eternity of raccoons and peacocks, hummingbirds and ravens, pumas

Allí solamente había árboles y gente. Allí terminaban la vida y la muerte. Allí comenzaba una eternidad de pinos y gansos salvajes, águilas y cedros, golondrinas y sicomoros, osos y halcones. De allí los salmones zarpaban hacia el Japón, conocían el Asia y se regresaban al rincón donde habían nacido. Por su costa pasaban las ballenas entonando un canto a los amores lejanos. Y allí continuaba otra eternidad de mapaches y pavos reales, picaflores y cuervos, pumas y sauces, olmos, llamas, truchas, patos, zaragüellas y salmones.

-Y tambien náguales -aseguró doña Asunción.

-¿Cómo dijo?- preguntó Gabriel- Oh, sí náguales. Pues qué mala suerte que Doroteo no se quiera levantar porque eso nos va a retardar un poquito. Lo que pensaba era ir con ustedes al aeropuerto, recibir a Elisa y seguir el viaje de allí nomás hacia Oregon.

-Espérate un momentito- dicen que dijo doña Asunción. Todo lo que se sabe es eso, pero nadie está seguro.

-Anda arrancando esa máquina- aseguran otros que dijo, y que entró en el cuarto de su hijo. ¿Qué le diría? No se sabe. ¿Cuánto tiempo hablaría? ¿Hablarían? No se puede decir. Algunos comentan que lo amenazó con castigarlo. Otros sostienen que le habló de los bosques de Oregon donde la gente encontraba su nágual y su sombra, donde el espacio entre árbol y árbol comenzaba a ser ocupado por el amor.

Otros aseguran que no fue así: dicen que la muerte llegó por fin a Berkeley y tocó la puerta, y que la señora Asunción le salió al frente, de mujer a mujer, de muerte a muerte, y que un pájaro comenzó a cantar, muy seguro de sí mismo, sobre un árbol de

and willows, elms, llamas, trouts, ducks, opossums and salmons again...

"And also naguales," assured doña Asunción.

"What did you say?"- he asked- "Oh, yes, naguales. But what bad luck it is that Doroteo does not want to get up because that is going to delay us a bit. What I was thinking was to go with you guys to airport, pick up Elisa, and continue our trip from there to Oregon."

"Wait a minute," said doña Asunción, according to some people who would retell the story. All that is known is that we do not know what happened. Nobody is sure what happened from that moment.

"Start the machine," the others assure she said, and she entered her son's room. What did she say to him? Nobody knows. How much time did she speak? Did they speak? It could not be said for sure. Some comment that she threatened him with punishment. Others maintain that she spoke of the forests of Oregon where the people can find their nagual and their shadow, where the space between tree and tree is occupied by love.

Others assured that it was not so: that Death finally arrived at Berkeley and knocked on the door. Doña Asunción went out to the front to meet her, woman to woman, face to face. A bird began to sing, very sure of himself, until the tree where he was perched was converted into a shadow and into oblivion.

The truth is that they went with the angel Gabriel. Don Adriano Leon swears that he saw mother and son walk out, slow and sure, in slow motion and enter the long motor home. What they are

enfrente hasta que la muerte se fuera y el árbol se convirtiera en sombra y en olvido.

La verdad es que se fueron con el ángel Gabriel. Por lo menos eso es lo que dicen que dijo don Adriano León quien vio a la madre y al hijo salir corriendo, lentos y seguros, como en cámara lenta e ingresar en la casa rodante. Lo que todos están seguros es que, mucho tiempo después de que el carro se hubo hundido en el horizonte, un resplandor de muchos colores los siguió flotando sobre el camino. Lo que otras personas dicen es que se los llevó un ángel, y punto.

all sure of is that, long after the motor train plunged into the horizon, a glitter of many colors followed it floating over the road.

Glossary

Arjun(es).- In Guatemala, Chamans.

Coyote.- Smuggler of inmigrants. Guide.

Gringo.- In South America, foreigner or national with green or blue eyes, or blond hair. It is only a descriptive term. In Mexico, U.S. citizen.

Nagual: From Maya mythology, belief in a double of animal nature.
Master: In this case, Chaman.

Testimony

Jasmine Cuddigan, Virginia Oliveros, Josefina
Zazueta, Christina Wyatt, Patricia Oliver, Alfie Linn,
René Holmes, Angel Namhie, Silvia Gómez,
Gretchen Idsinga, Amy Seloover, Ann Siebenmorgen,
Luisa Jaramillo, Christina Wendling

Things about family and love

Jasmine Cuddigan

This term, I was an English tutor at the cultural center near my home in Cornelius and I worked with four people. There names are Enrique, Rosendo, Modesto, and Hector. I have really enjoyed working with them and I probably learned more from them that they did from me. Not things about Spanish, but things about the personal characteristics of these four people things about Mexico and the people from Mexico, things about family and love. I have been a volunteer tutor at the Centro Cultural since January and I love it. I love learning about other cultures and helping them to understand my culture. I enjoy given my time because I get so much in return. This is nothing to give when one receives knowledge an understanding of something new.

I interviewed Enrique Placito because he is the student that seems to have the most free time in between working and taking English classes. At centro Cultural, English classes are offered and the students study two nights a week for two hours each night. I was a tutor one night a week for two hours and I also gave extra English classes at my house anytime one of my student needed them. One day I spent four hours at the porch in the sun with Hector. Who took turns reading out of his book, and we learned the days of the week and the months of the year. We spoke Spanish and English and this made us both laugh and have a good time. It was neat for us both to see how hard it is to speak in our non-native language. It was like magic, because we could communicate with what little we both knew. Hector told me how to make some of the special food that they make at his home in Mexico and told me all about his home, his family and his friends. It was so interesting and we both learned a lot.

Enrique and I have been hanging out a lot out of class too. We have gone to dinner and once to the big dance at the Convention Center. One day I had him over to my house for dinner which was, I'm sure, a very strange experience for him. We had asparagus, salad, bread with homous, and corn on the cob. He said he had never eaten asparagus before. It was fun to have him over though and I'm sure it was a new experience for him. All the while, Enrique and I are both learning a lot about people from different worlds.

Enrique came to Oregon with nothing. He had no job, no food, no car, no place to live or anything. He thanks god for the Centro Cultural where he ate and began his life here in Oregon. Now he had a good job, he had a place to live, he bought a car, and he even has enough money to send home to his sister and his family in Mexico. Enrique came here to the United States to work. He came out of necessity not out of desire to get to know the people of our country. He also came to learn English so he can be more marketable for jobs in Mexico. He thinks that here people are very close and selfish and that we worry about a lot of things that are unimportant. He says that in Mexico people are not worried about so many things

and in Mexico can live a more tranquil life than here where even the people that do have money don't enjoy themselves or live happy lives. The people here want everything for themselves and don't want to help other people.

Enrique is proud to be from Mexico and would never want to be from here. He always tells me how beautiful his home is and beautiful his family is. I think we could all learned a lesson from this. We have a beautiful country that many people could care less about. I think we have forgotten how lucky we are to have such a beautiful and fairly peaceful nation to call home. We have lost our pride and we should try to get it back. It's funny, because many people say "Mexican" with a derogatory tone in their voice, but those people have missed the beauty of the Mexican people and their culture and their pride. Those people have missed the sense of love, morals, family values, religious beliefs, honesty, and wonder that surrounds these people and define who they are. We need to take a closer look at their hearts and their souls. We need to see their passion for being alive that has die in many of us. Enrique says that he feels like a bird locked in a cage here. He is right, many of us are like birds locked in cages. We are locked up by our materialistic desires and our ignorant view about the rest of the world. We live in a small place called Oregon and we think this is life. I've news for everyone and that is that Oregon is just one rain drop on the windshield and is easy lost with one swipe of the blade.

Enrique works seven days a week for eight or more hours a day. He also takes English classes two nights a week. He also manages to have fun and go to dances with his other Mexican friends. Enrique sends money home to take care of his sisters and brothers because his mother died a year ago and his father is an alcoholic. Now, how many of us North Americans have the nobility to sacrifice ourselves like that? How many of us would go away from everything we love and live for in order to provide for our families? How many of us would give everything we have to help someone else? These people are beautiful and they have pride. They deserve some recognition rather than neglect.

Enrique says that it has been very hard to live here without his family, but that he will stay here and work, because his family needs him. He has had a hard time with not knowing English, but he is learning very quickly. He does not know much about the United States except that he lives and works in Oregon, so he did not want to judge our country without enough knowledge.

I would really recommend to everyone that they go out and volunteer to work with these people. You will have an eye-opening experience and you will love what you see.

Cultural similarities: The dream of a better future

Virginia Oliveros

The family that I worked with is very similar to my family. The family that I worked with consisted of three people. Antonio, Pabla, and Elizabeth Madera. Antonio is 22 years old, Pabla is 19 years old, and little Elizabeth is 3 years old. The couple is very young. They live in an apartment in Independence. They have only live here in the United States for three years. Since both Antonio and Pablo don't speak fluent English, they have told me that since they have moved to the U.S. it has been hard for them to communicate with people everywhere they go. If they found someone who speaks Spanish, they feel safe and secure asking them for help.

Antonio and Pabla have been putting a lot of effort in wanting to learn a second language, especially English. They think it is very important for them to learn the language while living here in the U.S. Antonio wants to learn so that he can understand his boss and co-workers at work. Pablo wants to learn so that she can understand what the store clerk, doctor, or the pharmacist is asking her. Both are eager to learn because they think that its the only way they can survive in living here. Antonio and Pabla married at a young age. Antonio was 19, and Pabla was 16. They are both from the state of Zacatecas, Mexico. They did not finish High School. They only went to school until, they were both about 14.

Both Antonio and Pabla come from a large family. Their parents live in a small farm in a small town in Zacatecas. When they got married in Mexico, Antonio had the desire of getting a good job, and giving the best of his wife, Pabla. He had heard from his brother, who lives in Salem, that Oregon was a great place to live, because they were many jobs available to Migrant people. He had the desire to work to give the best to his wife, and to send the many to his mother and father so that they could save money to build a better home for them and the rest of Antonio's younger brothers and sisters. He says that he would like his parents to have a better living by helping them in any way that he can.

Pabla tells me that she is very proud of her husband because of all the effort he has done to help the family. Their three years old daughter is the one important thing in their life along with their parents, too. They both have worked very hard to raise their daughter. Their dream is for Elizabeth to go to College. When I first met them and I told them that I was at WOSC, they were delighted in asking me how I got to where I am today and what they needed to do if one day they decided on going to college. They want the best for their daughter. They have told me that they want Elizabeth to have the best future ever. They want her to be successful and be a doctor or a lawyer. But whatever she chooses to be they hope it will make her happy and successful.

Antonio and Pabla have

strong desires to learn English for a better future. they would like me to continue tutoring them. They think that the English language is interesting. They say that their biggest Cultural Shock was when the first arrive here in the United States, they were shocked at seeing that here in America, Americans pay things with checks or banks cards. Pabla says that she had never seen such a thing in the town she lived, until she moved here. She also said that people here use the automobile as a major way of transportation, unlike in Mexico people usually walk or ride their bikes in order to get to where they need to be. It was a shock to both Antonio and Pabla because they had never had a car in Mexico, until they bought one here in Oregon.

These are just a few things that they both think were shocking to them when they arrived to the U.S. is different from Mexico in some ways, but also there are things that they found quite similar in both countries. Antonio and Pabla have been living day by day a different Cultural environment. They enjoy it, but they say they miss their country. Even though they have found that here in Oregon they have met people from different parts of the Mexican Republic, and that they have found that they can find and do things.

Many of this similarities I can find in my family. My parents also have gone through the things and customs Antonio and Pabla have gone through. I feel that there are similarities in both my family and in the madera family. In find this very interesting. I find that there are cultural similarities in my family to the family I tutored. It was fun and enjoyable to converse in English and in Spanish with them. I have a fun time spending some hours sharing of my interests and knowledge with this family. I have never met them before, even though I've living in Independence, almost all my life. Now, I have new friends that live in my community That I can converse and visit from now on. I have gained some experience in getting to know other Hispanic people that live close to me. I enjoyed tutoring them, and I hope to continue with the tutoring program for a long time.

How to call for help

Josefina Zazueta

When I was first told that tutoring a Spanish family or person in the community was a requirement for my Spanish culture class, I was a little frightened but very excited. It seemed like a great opportunity to practice my Spanish and to meet someone from a different culture.

I am a first generation Hispanic in the United States, with parents from Mexico and Cuba, so I know many of the customs and traditions of Mexico. however not until I began tutoring did I realize the diversity of the Mexican people from region to region.

The woman I am tutoring lives in Salem, Or. with her husband, and three children. She and her family moved to Oregon from

Mexico nine years ago in order to make a better life for their children. She is a young mother with a son who is three years old, and a daughter who is nine and, another son who is twelve years old. Although her two older children and husband speak English, she and her three year old son do not. She doe not work outside of the home, nor know many people who speak English, and as result, she was a very limited vocabulary.

she has told me some of the problems that she faces as a result of not speaking English. For example, she does not know of many of the services in the community that are available to her and her family. She have been unable to find a work because she does not know of anyone she can leave her youngest son with, and because she does not have a driver's license.

She has wanted to learn English but has been afraid of taking formal classes in a school setting. She found out about the volunteer Spanish tutoring program at Cherokee through a friend, and felt that been taught English in her own home would be less frightening and more practical.

Another major problem that she and her husband faced deals with eldest son in school. He has been having problems in class, and because his teacher does not speak Spanish, it has been very difficult for him to communicate with him. If she wants to talk with someone from the school, she must wait for her husband to be present so he can translate for her.

Some basic concerns she has, and is interesting in learning about, deal with survival skills. For example, how to call for help if one of her children gets hurt, how to find a family doctor, where and how to get a driver's license, and how to fill out a job application, are just a few.

There is still a lot that she must learn and she still has many questions, but now there is someone who can help her get answers without feeling intimidated or afraid. I have enjoyed this experience so much that we are planing on continuing with it through the summer and keeping in touch thereafter. We have both learned a lot about our different cultures and we have also learned that we are not that different in may ways.

For José each new word was a jewel...

Christina Wyatt

I have worked for a period of nine weeks at the Polk County Housing Authority in Dallas tutoring English as a Second Language for Hispanic adults. Over this period of time I have worked with a number of students all eager to learn English. One students that I worked with consistently was Jose. Jose

and his wife and their three children (two girls and a boy) have lived in the U.S.A. for almost twenty years now. Their children were born in the U.S. and are in very way bilingual. Jose can both read and write Spanish as well as basic English (about third or fourth level). One of his favorite activities

was looking up words in the dictionary (a rather useful but mundane task to most American students). For Jose each word was a jewel that he treasured. He was quick use his new-found vocabulary the following tutor session to show me that he had been practicing at home.

I have learned a lot about the Hispanic culture in my short time with Jose. He told me about the first time that he and his wife came to the U.S. They had left Jalisco and lived in Mexico City for a short time before heading north to the U.S. Jose remembers that he and his wife had to pay $300 a piece to enter the country. Still Jose though it a small piece to pay to be able to live in the land of opportunity, the U.S. He recalls his visits to Mexico City where he remembers seeing twenty families living in a single room not much bigger than my bedroom. They lived without electricity most of the time, making refrigeration impossible; running water is considered a luxury. Jose chose not to raise a family in this conditions and continue north to the U.S., doing odd jobs or seasonal work to get the money for him and his wife to cross the border.

Still, Jose learn with the wonderment of a new born child. One of our big projects was to identify various countries in the map. Jose has never seen a map before our lessons. I was awed at how I had taken even that for granted. He knew the name of many countries but did not know their size and locations, so we explored the world and it was like I was seeing the

world for the first time as well. He marveled at how big the world was at yet how small. He laughs and smiles, after all who would have though that the world encounter so many of his fellow Mexicans in the U.S. Who would have though that he would find Americans who spoke Spanish. He smiles and notes how many Americans are learning to speak Spanish, and that is good he says. Now our culture can even be closer; we can be just more than neighbors, we can be friends.

Personally, I have found Jose and his family to be an inspiration. He is always eager to learn. During this final weeks it has often been just him and me in a large empty room taking about the world. He calls me "maestra" which made me a little nervous as I am young enough to be his daughter, but this is how she shows his respect. Many Americans argue that they do not want the migrant workers in the U.S., that they are disrespectful and ignorant. I have only think of Jose and his courage to leave behind everything he had ever known- his home, friends, his family, and many ways his culture and his language-to know that this is not true. Jose and my other students have shown me nothing but respect during my tutoring. They are grateful that I have taken the time to learn their language and they are happy to share their lives and their homes with me. I more American reach out, they too would experience the wonders of the Hispanic culture as I have during this project.

Cultural Diversity and Interaction benefit a community

Patricia Oliver

In the area of Monmouth-Independence, the combined population is relatively small, 10,000 residents, more or less. With the abundance of agriculture in this area, many Hispanics have come to work and many have stayed, adding to the wonderful culture of this part of Willamette Valley. It is estimated that in this area alone there are about 1,500 Hispanics.

In my opinion, they not only have added a cultural experience, but their help in the many facets of agriculture are vital. They work in areas of harvesting food for us that most of us would not be willing do. But many situations are difficult for them. Some of these situations, I explored with my student, Lourdes.

I feel it necessary to understand a bit of the background of this family in order to place their viewpoint in the overall picture. Jaime, a fine gentleman in my estimation, is a graduate of an horticulture school in Mexico. They came to the United States five or six years ago, but Jaime is not proficient in speaking English even though he reads and understands quite well. Lourdes was educated through the eighth grade in Mexico and has not spoken English, except for fragments when necessary. However, I am finding her not only intelligent, but very witty and can read and write all the necessary things in English. She is eager to learn and in teaching her I am finding what I have observed in other of the Hispanics that have been here for awhile. Their knowledge is spotty and incomplete. But with encouragement and an opportunity to be taught they can fill in the gaps of their knowledge, and become active citizens of our community.

Lourdes was reluctant to complain, but finally she spoke objectively about needs in the areas of translation, medical assistance, courts, transportation, housing and employment.

Lack of, or sporadic, work and lack of sufficient English are the forefront of the other problems. Lack of translators in the courts and medical facilities are a major problem. If the Hispanics have the money, they can obtain local medical assistance. But there is not one to translate for them. So the majority of the ill must go to Salem for aid. And in Salem there are increasing changes to contend with. For example, a West Salem Clinic used to take them, but now only accepts pregnant women. La Clinica Guadalupe costs $20 per visit for their services, and they do speak Spanish. But for this or other clinics that might help, one must have access to a car or find someone available to take them. Often the Saavedras assist them as there is no local transportation system.

For many, housing shortage and money are a problem and it results in many people living together in small crowded quarters. Often the result of this is the agitation of people and, according to Lourdes, the woman end up yelling at one other, something that

bothers her.

What happens is a family is desperately in need of food or clothes? I asked. Sometimes St. Patrick's Church helps out and they can go to the local "soup kitchen", she explained.

Jaime and Lourdes came here in hopes of having a better life and a better education for their only child. She is doing exceptionally well in school and they think highly of the local school system as well as the community. However, they may have to move to Portland, even though they like it here, because they are told there is more employment there. Jaime is a very capable, knowledgeable and hardworking individual. They don't complain, but they are having a difficult time. They miss their family in Mexico, but for them a good education for their daughter is important.

I questioned my student about the problem of prejudice which we some-times hear about, and her remarks was that they didn't find much problem, but when it did occur it was usually from the Chicanos, meaning the American born Hispanics.

Not all foreigners are a tax burden

Alfie Linn

In the case of my family, the most serious problem that they encountered when they arrived to the U.S., for the first time was not being able to find housing. The señora told me that when she and her family (husband and kids) first arrived, they had no place to live and did not know if they would be able to find work. They did not, however, that life in the U.S. had to be better than what life offered in their own country. When they preferred to be in their own country, they had no choice but to take the chances elsewhere.

The main problem according to the señora was that because she did not speak English, she had way of communicating her needs. She felt that people here in the U.S. were not receptive to her problem of not being able to speak in English nor to her needs. It was not as she wanted every person to help her, but she did not understood the distance that Americans put between Latin Americans (especially Mexicans).

To make things worse the señora and her family found themselves victims of the American society. This is to say that they had to deal with the biased opinions of Americans towards Mexicans. She felt that Americans in general regarded Mexicans as tax burdens because they would drain the funds of a social service program such as welfare. This, however, is true. Some Mexicans (foreigners) take advantage of the system and simply live off the government. Yet at the same time, these people have to pay taxes for work just as we do, and in comparison, according to several case studies, the foreigners pay more taxes to the government than does the government pay them in services.

Another problem the family experienced was not being able to

use the money system to their advantage. Even today, after being here for years, this family can not recognize the money values. This is to say that the señora can go to the store and not be able to understand how much things cost. She will buy what she needs, not taking in account of how much things cost and not being able to look for the better buys. One would argue that this is completely stupid. However, due to the fact that no one has tough to this people how to use the money, and not being able to ask someone who knows, it is not a big surprise that they have not learned. This is a serious problem because here you have these people working probably for below minimum wage, spending money to do things that could be found cheaper elsewhere if the knew the difference.

Personally, I feel that these people do need help and they need it now. I am pleased to know that there are at least some programs that these people can turn to, but by not mean there is enough services for the demands. I do not feel is the responsibility of Americans to take care of every immigrant who decides to come to the U.S., but at least we can offer some assistance to those people that are honest workers, people that have no choice but to leave their of life and embark on a non-promising future in a foreign country.

Caught by the neck

René Holmes

When asked what his first impression of the United States was, José, a very dedicated student of English, took no time in answering. It was clear that his first impression was also a big impression: immigration. He had come across the border to work seasonally and ended up being chased through the same fields he had been working. An immigration officer had caught him by the neck and pulled him to a stop; he was promptly shipped back to Mexico.

This setback didn't deter Jose in any way; he continued to come to the States to work the various harvests and returning to Mexico every year during the interim. He eventually met and married his wife while back home. They moved to the States around 1979, and a year ago, he had taken no initiative to learn English; he hadn't needed to. He had spent his time in the fields or with his family, both were Spanish was spoken. He mentioned that any court situation for an immigrant was trying (no pun intended) because of the language barriers. He also has had problems communicating with the boss on occasion, however, he has started taking steps to remedy the situation.

He had two accidents in the early 1980's that caused him to later need two back surgeries. He still suffers form pain and loss of work. Every week during the tutoring sessions he must take a break to stand and walk around in order to stretch his back. Also in the same period of time he had open heart surgery. He feels that because of his medical conditions,

his life has changed. He has greater appreciation for his family and himself. He now prefers to work and care for his family over everything there.

With his move to the U.S., he was offered a new future. He saw new opportunities and a life that he could have not achieved in Mexico. He hadn't school while growing up and that had kept him from earning enough money in his native country to be able to support a family. The move also offered his children a better education, medical attention among the many other programs to aid the people.

His family consists of about 130 people...

Angel Namhie

Pablo and Julie Orozco are from Zacatecas, Mexico. Pablo owns a 1,000 acre ranch in Mexico, but he does not own any animals and as result, his family does not have much money or food. His whole family, which consist of about 130 people, lives and works on this ranch, but the harsh dry climate doe not allow for fertile land and, therefore, it does not produce enough crops to support such a large number of people.

There is no schooling for the children who live in Zacatecas; however Pablo feels the education is extremely important for his family. In fact, it is so important to him that he moved his family to the U.S. Seven of his nine children are attending school now and his five year old is being tutored by a lady who speaks both English and Spanish.

Pablo came over first, and when he got here he did not know English. He repeatedly listen to people speaking so he could learn the language.

Gradually, he learned enough to get by from listening to the people around him. Julia, who came over later, still does not speak English. She knows a little, but he still feels very timid about speaking.

When they arrived in the United States, they felt there were many opportunities and benefits which would help them raise their family. Education was the first and foremost on their mind, but Pablo could also work and provide a good home and enough food for the family. Julia feels that it is great that her children can be educated and she wants them to be whatever they desire. Pablo and Julia are excited about their life in the United States, However they worry about the people in Mexico who do not have enough food to eat and the kids go without education. But they both hope that government in Mexico will soon begin to develop a system to help provide for these needy families. They believe bringing more industrial business into Mexico would help the people get away from the shaky business of agriculture.

Enough money to be able to go back to Mexico

Silvia Gómez

The woman's name is Josefina Muñoz. She is the proud mother of two very young children. She has a son and a daughter. Then son's name is Felix, and the daughter's name is Shayla. Felix is two and Shayla is three years old. Josefina is only twenty eight years old. I never got to meet her husband because he was always at work. He works for the timber industry for the state of Oregon. That is why he is never home, he is always driving to Washington, or even California. He leaves for about three weeks at a time. I noticed when I saw the children that they are very sad because dad is always gone away.

She gets very lonely because they are the only Hispanic family if Falls City. I think that we have become good friends ever since I have been teaching her English, even her two children learn some words when we get together.

Josephine is a very determined young woman. She lived a very bad life in Mexico because her family had very little money. Actually, they had no money at all. She came from a very big family, and she too wants to have a very big family here in the states. She said that she feels bad because sometimes people try to talk to her but she has a bad accent and they make fun of her all the time. I told her to not worry and keep on practicing what I have taught her. The good thing about this woman is that she is very determined about everything, especially about learning English. She plans on going back to Mexico and teaching it to her family. I told Josefina when I met her, that I would teach her English but that it was not going to be easy at all. I told her that she had to be very patient, and just to have fun with it. She told me she wanted to learn enough to be able to get a good job here in Oregon. She wants to help her husband make just enough money to be able to go back to Mexico.

In the past six weeks that I have been with Josefina, she has learned many new words and phrases. She can now greet people properly on her own. She also knows words for asking for things. and how to ask for them properly. She knows many new words for foods, and words for when they travel. Her biggest problem she told me was to answer the phone. She told me that she would get very timid because the people could not understand her at all. So many times she would hang up on some important phone calls. And her husband would get mad because he would call from far away and no one would answer the phone.

This would make him worry and he would get mad because he would call from far away. I taught her some basic phone call lines such as "hello", "who's calling", and "he can't come to the phone now", "can I take a message", and other phrases to. She also had a problem with going shopping because she would never know how much money to give the person at the cash register. We studied numbers from one to thirty five. They were hard for her to learn at first, but she got the hang of it.

We even went shopping one day, and she did a very good job. She said "how much is it?" I was so proud of her because I knew this would be very hard to do. We went out to dinner and she asked for almost everything on her own. She still gets really shy when she talks to Americans, especially when she talks to men. She thinks that they will giggle at her. I just tell her that they normally don't do that, not unless they like you!

I have seen Josefina's English grow so much in these past few weeks. I am very proud of her be-cause she does want to make a good change for herself. I get mad when I see a lot of new Hispanic people and they don't want to learn anything. They just want everything to come easy to them. I wish that there was more deter-mined people like Josefina. Then there would be more Hispanics progressing in the state. Josefina has also grown a lot as a person. She has a lot of confidence that she did not before. I am really happy that I was able to meet her and teach her something that she is going to use for the rest of her life.

Who they really are

Gretchen F. Idsinga

In the beginning of this term I was not quite aware of how significant the English tutoring that I was doing for my Spanish 339 class, Introduction to Latin-American Culture, would play on my greater understanding of this culture and its peoples.

Though I was born in the United States I have never really considered myself to be an Ameri-can because of the fact I have only lived in this country one-third of my entire life. My parents moved to Columbia, South America when I was eleven years old, so I grew up much like a young Colombian girl, and would gladly accept to call myself Colombian if someone did not believe I was an American. I not only lived in Columbia for almost nine years, but also in Guatemala City, Guatemala for two years, as well as the Navajo Indian Reservation in Arizona for two years, and one year in Russia. Knowing this, you could say that I am a world citizen, and probably somewhat of a mixture of all the cultures I have lived it.

The women I have been working with, Maria and her daughter, Sara have been very en-joyable. When I first started going to their home in Monmouth they were somewhat shy and reserved, which is natural, but slowly as we got to know each other they be-came much more open to asking me questions as well as relaxed and comfortable as they struggles with certain words or phrases.

Part of being able to teach anyone anything is to get to know their personality and learning style, so of course part of this is to become more aware of their cul-ture and in this case, family dy-namics. I soon noted that Maria was more assertive, though when she did not know something I was asking, Sara always helped her. Sara, on the other hand was very shy in the beginning, but has

118

warmed up a lot now that we know each other.

Guadalupe, Maria's husband, though not officially part of the class, because he is often at work all day, if he is home, tends to linger in the background probably listening and taking mental notes with the hopes that he will also learn some English.

To go on I must describe the home they live in. Maria, Guadalupe and Sara live in the upstairs portion of a house on the outskirts of Monmouth. One of Maria's brothers lives downstairs with his wife and two-year-old son, and in the house next door, live another on of Maria's brothers and his children. Maria, her husband and daughter share close quarters in the upstairs portion of the house, which is composed on one large room and possibly a bathroom behind a curtain, but it could just be a storage area. Downstairs on the back porch is a sink where they wash their dishes, and in the front hallway of the house before you get to the stairs is the stove on the right-hand side, and the refrigerator on the left, blocking most of the space in front of the stairs, so that I must remove my backpack to get through. Everything is neat and tidy and always clean, and they always welcome me with smiling faces. Upstairs they have a small television in Spanish, a couple of different clocks, a telephone, a few pictures in frames on the walls, a large calendar, shelves where they have everything arranged nicely, a dresser, a sofa, a single bed and a double bed, and a chair or two.

Maria's and her family have been living in Monmouth for two years, and it is the only place they have lived in the United States. Sara and her mother have previously worked taking care of children, but right now Sara is working as a cleaning lady at a hotel here in Monmouth, and Maria takes care of the household chores, shopping and cooking, though she says she would like to get a job. Guadalupe works on a Christmas tree farm somewhere outside Salem where he keeps them trimmed and looking nice. These are very honest and hardworking people.

They say they do like the United States though they do miss Mexico and their other family members. Maria and Guadalupe have another daughter that still lives in Mexico, as well as Maria's mother. Maria comes from a family of twelve so having family close by is important. One of her sisters and her family live in Independence and they see each other frequently. Also, because they do have lots of friends and family close by they keep up with some of the "Latin-American" traditions such as the very important "quinceañera", which is a party to celebrate the fifteenth birthday of a young girl. This is second only to her wedding. They showed me photographs in which they were all dressed up at the church for this special occasion for one of their friends.

It is very important and positive that they have a close network of friends and family as a support system, because moving to and living in a foreign country is very difficult, and even more difficult if you do not have people around you that understand who you are and what you are going through. I assured them through my experiences in Russia, that they were not alone in their struggles; that I went through many of the same things. Part of their adjustment to living

here is keeping their culture and language which is who they really are, and adopting this culture slowly as they learn more and more about it.

The time I have spent with Maria and Sara has been somewhat of a sharing and finding similarities between our lives, sharing our life circumstances of my husband's job in Eugene, and Guadalupe's job outside of Salem, as well as Sara's job here in Monmouth, my schooling and Maria's daily responsibilities. It has been mostly a discovery of our similarities, and a sharing as we all try to live our lives in the most productive way possible, and learn to live the best we can wherever we are.

Over all I have learned more about myself

Amy E. Seloover

This term I worked with two Mexican women living in Independence, Maria and Elena. They called me "maestra," a term I was somewhat embarrassed by in the beginning. I learned to accept the fact that , is what I am to them, and I learned to play the part. I set up plans for lessons that would go a completely different direction and, at times, I felt like I wasn't teaching anything at all. It was really frustrating. The progress I've seen in each of them pleases and convinces me that they will go far if they continue in this tutoring program.

I was actually "assigned" to Elena, but when I got there the first time, Maria was there and interested in lessons too. Linda tested Maria to place her at a level and found that she was a couple of levels higher than Elena and would probably have to wait for a tutor. I ended up being that tutor because I didn't want her to wait when she was so willing to learn. The hour every Tuesday and Thursday, usually extended by half and hour or so, was split between them both. I wished I had more time for them, but I was already so busy with my own classes. That was probably the most frustrating point of all. I knew if I had more time they could learn more.

Maria has been in the US for about 19 years in California and Oregon. She knows English well enough to communicate and function in the community but wanted to practice the past tense. She has nine children, the youngest in Kindergarten and the oldest a senior in high school. I only met two of them due to illness and heard tidbits about the rest. Maria spoke lovingly and fondly about them all. She appeared to be so at home with raising such a large family, going to church on Sundays and expanding her horizons learning to speak and understand English better. She has also begun English night classes two nights a week, so she has more from which to learn.

Just last week Elena's little boy was sick so Maria and I had to hour to ourselves. We sat and talked almost the entire time. She talked about her children and the differences among them and how being a mother was so important. She said that her children always

come first in her life, then her husband and then herself. We talked about the responsibilities a person, or two people, has when they bring kids into this world. It totally and completely changes the one's world and adds the strongest connection to this new life.

I think that people, the uneducated, ignorant part of our society, believes that anyone who is not of the same race or color is strange, odd, or abnormal. I don't believe that and abhor anyone who does, and this conversation proved that no matter where you come from you still have feeling of love and anger and bitterness and happiness. You still have traditions and beliefs that run from the soul and they are not so different from the people around you regardless of color or race or origin. When I am a "real" teacher someday, I will tell this story in hopes of emphasizing the unique quality we all share. Maria has taught me well.

Elena is 24 years old and has two small children, Ans. age 3, and Jorge, nine months. Elena has been in Independence for less than two years and came from the south of Mexico. Elena is just beginning to learn English. I admire her for trying and making mistakes and trying again. Like all of us there are days which we really don't feel like learning or talking, but Elena seemed to try during all of the time we spent. Elena is quiet and reserved but willing to learn. The first lessons we had together, we made flash cards with pictures of food and colors mostly. It seemed to be going slowly, but at the beginning of each lesson we reviewed and she was catching on. I tend to think that I used too much English with her too soon. I also think that she needed the full hour of each lesson to encourage her to speak and understand.

If I had to do it over again, we would have gone outside for more "hands on" activities. "Across the street," would have meant more if only we would have gone across an actual street. We held classed in Maria's house and I wonder if the lesson would have had more impact if more lessons had been at Elena's.

Overall, I have learned more about myself and more about the Mexican culture. This program can help so much if there are people to staff it. I have pondered the lives of these two women over the past weeks and found that I admire anyone who would pick up and leave familiar surroundings for a better, possibly more difficult life. They came not knowing who and what they might find, but came anyway. They are trying to become more involved in their community by learning the language. I knew that English was suppose to be a hard language to learn, but I never realized exactly how hard until now. Why are words spelled the way they are yet sound completely different?

Grammar still needs a lot of work

Ann Siebenmorgen

My student's name is Leopoldo Pascal from Independence, Oregon. He has lived in the United States for about 7-8 years, I think, in and out of different states until now living here in Oregon. Throughout most of this term we have met about two days a week for about two hours each day at the park here in Monmouth. He has said many times that it is so difficult, because it is very challenging in every aspect.

I started out with asking him basic vocabulary, and them he brought sets of words that he wanted me to translate. He said that overall everything was a problem for him. He can speak quite a bit English but a lot of it's pretty general. Usually he can understand some English too, but I find myself speaking slower so that he can understand it. It is also hard for him to ask basic questions. He copes by just taking it day by day and learning things as he does them. Experience is a major way of his learning.

I asked him if he goes home and practices hes reading and vocabulary, but he said that there is a lot of people there and it is hard to concentrate. That is why it is nice to be able to go to a tutor that will force him to practice it.

Grammar and sentence structure still needs a lot of work, because although we did do some of that, we did not get everything covered. I believe that he has been through nine to ten years of school in Mexico so he is still learning things in his own language.

Most of the time he is pretty good with pronunciation with the occasion of sometimes pronouncing vowels different. he is very willing and determined to learn and will often repeat many times until he gets it right. One thing that we did not really focus on was me dictating words and him writing them down. He didnot get to much practice doing that just because it did not seem as important to him as important to him as the other key parts like pronunciation, reading, vocabulary, and sentence structure.

One thing that is a really good idea is taking the student on different excursions. One time we went to the Market Place to identify certain fruits and vegetables and name them as we went. It helped him associate what he was thinking to English. We also took a little trip to the Coffee Shop where he was forced to ask for what he wants. This was very hard for him so I had to help him a little. So in these types of situations he needs to learn to do it himself although he is struggling with it. But so far he has learned to deal with it which is commendable.

Overall, he is concerned with every little aspect and is interested in gaining a much better understanding of the language.

She writes poetry

Luisa Jaramillo

The student that I worked with is very intelligent. I originally expected her to not be able to speak English, but I soon learned I was wrong, she not only speaks English, but she is able to translate her poetry into English as well.

She arrived in Oregon with her two sons about eight months age. She now lives in Independence and works for a nursery. When she first arrived in the United States her main obstacle was the language. She says that she has learned over the years that all people are the same. The didnot notice any big differences here from her native country Mexico. She says that she likes living in the United States and the people are very friendly.

She expresses herself a lot through her poetry and I have been fortunate enough to have been able to read some of her poems.

She is a very busy woman. After working all day she comes home to take care of her two sons ages fifteen and eighteen. She loves to listen to music and listens to the radio as much as she can. Her two favorite American artist are Maria Carey and Whitney Houston. She is very involved with her church, St. Hilda's in Independence. She wrote a poem in honor of all the mothers in the church for Mother's Day. She has also started a youth organization in the church called "Los Jovenes Obreros Cristianos". She is very concerned about the Hispanic youth in Independence. She wants to help them retain their culture and language and provide them with a support group. She moved to Oregon so she and her children could realize their dreams. She has always wanted to become a missionary, but had never been able to realize that dream, until now. She says that she will be a missionary here in Oregon.

She has a strong desire to improve her English. Her boss discovered that she could speak English so she asked her to be the translator between her and the other workers. After working all day she still takes the time to meet with me every Wednesday and Thursday night to practice her English. She is using English more and more every day. By this time next year she would be an expert speaker !

She is a very brave and intelligent woman with a lot of dreams and aspirations that are coming true for both her and her two sons.

North Americans basically have the same hearts as Latin Americans...

Cristina Wendling

When I started with this program for non-native English speakers I was not sure what to expect. After having one session with my student I was reassured that this program would not only help her, but myself as well.

My student is in a very unique situation. She is a middle-aged single mother with two teenaged children. That in itself is not unique, but she also has had thirteen years of education in Veracruz, Mexico. Naturally after finding this bit of information out i asked what kind of job she has here in the United States. She is a worker at a local plant nursery. She can speak some conversational English so she told me about her experience when she came here to the Pacific Northwest.

She arrived here from Veracruz, Mexico about ten months ago. Only knowing a limited amount of English she started to look for job. She found an opening at a nursery, and gladly accepted the welcome work. She works eight to ten hours a day, without complaining. After she moved herself and her two children into a trailer house, she tried to settled. She had to enroll one of her sons in the local high school and learn how to use the post office and other social serves that are offered here.

Her first impression of North American- Caucasian people was that they were a little on the cold side. After she found a church she liked that preconception changed. The church really helped her to get acquainted with a wide range of people. Now she has many friends who are form Latin America as well as North America born friends. The church helped her to be able to become really good friends and learn mopre about North Americans,

She also had a prejudged notion that all North Americans were rich and played baseball. After being here awhile she has realized that this is not the case. She then stated that North Americans basically have the same hearts as Latin Americans but they express their feelings differently. This is one part of life here that still puzzles her. She is still not sure whwn it is appropiate to say or how she should express her feelings to not offend people. Being an Oregonian this would not crossed my mind as diffrence between our two cultures. Every once in a while she will tell me a situation that happened to her at work, to find out what the proper way of responding should be. She always has a smile on her face no matter what has happened.